INTRODUCTION

These **20 dog-friendly walks** have been designed to give both dogs and their human companions a wonderful time exploring the beautiful Lancashire countryside and coastline. All will be a delight to your best friend, whether romping on the shoreline at St Annes or roaming the saltmarshes at Hest Bank, trekking over open moorland up to the Peel monument high over the Irwell valley, or sampling the freedom of woodland and stream-side rambling. There is always something of human interest too, from ancient churches such as lovely St Mary-le-Ghyll to Roman remains at Ribchester and Second World War reminders at Anglezarke and Healey Dell. Medieval dewponds, canal towpaths, steam trains and country parks in the centre of town, such as Towneley Park in Burnley, all add to the enjoyment.

The routes not only produce a spread of locations around Lancashire but also provide a variation in the distance covered and difficulty of terrain. I have enjoyed the company of a trio of black Labradors over more than 30 years and young animals need more exercise than older animals. These walks have been planned bearing in mind that doggie stamina will vary from breed to breed.

Those who write guide books are increasingly meeting with a problem. Most authors give route instructions and starting points by reference to pubs. With the recent economic problems many country hostelries are closing down and are either becoming derelict or are now private dwellings. To me this means two things: firstly, I try to patronise hostelries which allow well-behaved dogs to enter in order to support their future; secondly, I play safe by taking with me a canine picnic, a supply of water and a good sturdy towel. Each walk has suggestions for places to find refreshments, or where would be a good place to stop and eat al fresco.

Walking is always a pleasure when the weather is fine and sunny but dog owners have to go out in all conditions. Whenever I hear the wind blowing and the rain sweeping down, I listen to my dog, play my well-worn CD of George Gershwin's *Walking the Dog* and reach for my boots, coat and car keys. Having a dog is a reason for not being lazy and I am grateful to each and every one of my walking companions. I hope you and your dog get as much enjoyment from these walks as I have.

Ron Freethy

ADVICE FOR DOG WALKERS

'Having a dog provides a great excuse for taking a walk. The benefits of getting out and about in the fresh air with your four-legged friend are many, so enjoy the rewards and happy dog walking.' *(This and the basis for the advice that follows comes from the Natural England website: www. naturalengland.org.uk)*

Dogs bring so much enjoyment to their owners but being in charge of a dog does bring with it some responsibilities. Whilst many people welcome seeing dogs, owners should be aware that not all walkers like to have canine interruptions, especially those who are engaged in other 'sports' such as orienteering, horse riding, jogging and especially anglers and birdwatchers so do respect their privacy and ensure your dog is not annoying anyone.

Care should also be taken to appreciate the importance of farmland so don't allow your dog to run loose and do remember to close any gates after you have passed through. If you should find yourself surrounded by inquisitive and possibly aggressive cattle, let the dog off the lead and leave the situation as quickly as possible. Your dog has four legs and can escape more easily than you can. Once these factors are borne in mind then dog walking can be really enjoyable.

Don't forget to take a drink and a dry towel, plus a doggie picnic if you are planning to have a mid-walk snack and, of course, remember to take a good supply of poo bags. If there is no bin to hand for easy disposal, please don't leave them behind for others to find but take them with you and dispose of them responsibly.

ACKNOWLEDGEMENTS

With grateful thanks to Roger, the German shepherd, Gizmo, the Welsh collie, and the trio of black Labradors Sabre, Bono and Inka.

Inka was given her name as we bought her after walking the Inca Trail in Peru. As a writer I use lots of black ink and so we altered the 'c' to a 'k'!

With thanks to Marlene who chose all our four-legged friends and to these eager dogs who forced us to get out and enjoy the countryside.

Lancashire

A DOG WALKER'S GUIDE

Ron Freethy

COUNTRYSIDE BOOKS
NEWBURY BERKSHIRE

First published 2011
Revised and updated 2014
© Ron Freethy 2011

COUNTRYSIDE BOOKS
3 Catherine Road
Newbury, Berkshire

To view our complete range of books,
please visit us at
www.countrysidebooks.co.uk

ISBN 978 1 84674 236 1

Photographs by the author

Cover photograph supplied by
Roger Evans

Designed by Peter Davies, Nautilus Design
Produced through The Letterworks Ltd., Reading
Typeset by Jean Cussons Typesetting, Diss, Norfolk
Printed by Berforts Information Press, Oxford

Contents

Introduction   5
Advice for Dog Walkers   6
🐾 Acknowledgements   6

Walk

1 Warton Crags *(2 miles)* 8
2 Hest Bank and Bolton-le-Sands *(4½ miles)* 13
3 Stocks Reservoir *(7 miles)* 17
4 Slaidburn and Croasdale Brook *(4 miles)* 22
5 Gisburn *(4 miles)* 26
6 Knott End *(5 miles)* 31
7 Greenberfield Locks and Barnoldswick *(4 miles)* .36
8 Calder Vale *(2 miles)* 40
9 Around Fairhaven Lake, St Annes *(2½ miles)* 44
10 Barley *(4 miles)* 48
11 Ribchester, Stydd and Kellets *(4½ miles)* 53
12 Towneley *(2½ miles)* 58
13 Clowbridge and Gambleside *(2 miles)* 63
14 Around Roach Bridge *(3½ miles)* 67
15 Hoghton *(3 miles)* 71
16 Anglezarke and Clough *(3½ miles)* 75
17 White Coppice *(3 miles)* 79
18 Around Healey Dell *(2 miles)* 83
19 Holcombe Moor and Ramsbottom *(5½ miles)* ...87
20 Smithills Country Park *(2 miles)* 92

Appendix

🐾 Contact details for veterinary practices close
to the walks   96

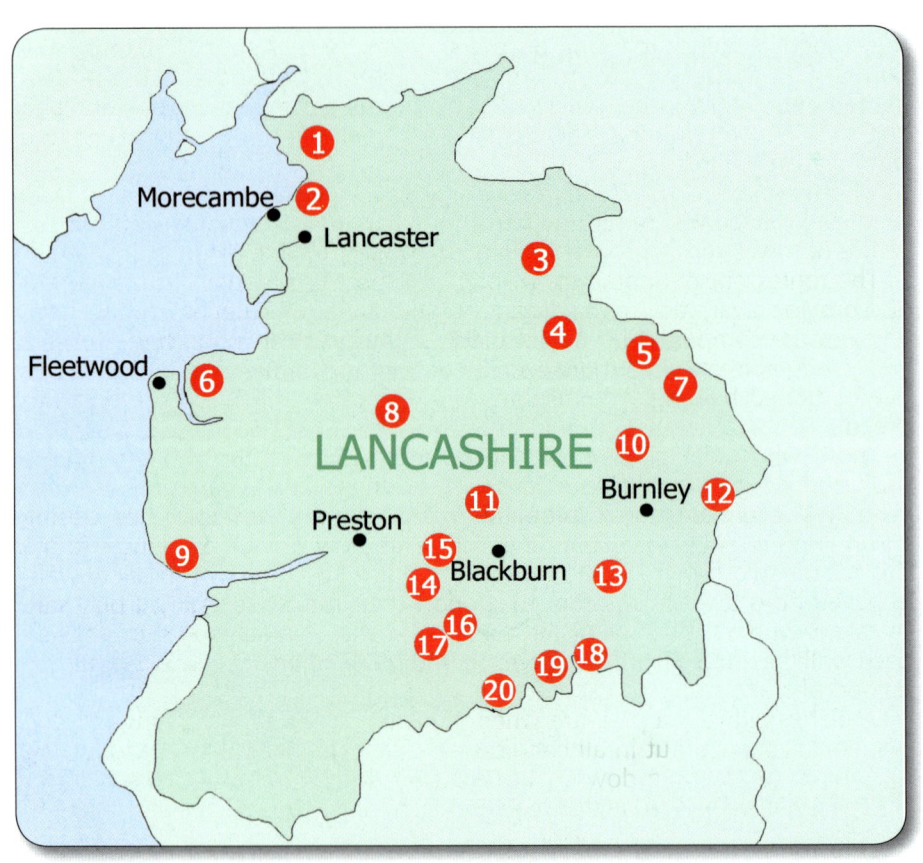

Area map showing location of the walks.

PUBLISHER'S NOTE

We hope that you obtain considerable enjoyment from this book. Although at the time of publication all routes followed public rights of way or permitted paths, diversion orders can be made and permissions withdrawn.

We cannot, of course, be held responsible for such diversion orders and any inaccuracies in the text which result from these or any other changes to the routes, nor any damage which might result from walkers trespassing on private property. We are anxious though that all details covering the walks are kept up to date and would therefore welcome information from readers which would be relevant to future editions.

The simple sketch maps that accompany the walks in the book are based on notes made by the author whilst checking out the routes on the ground. For the benefit of a proper map, however, we do recommend that you purchase the relevant Ordnance Survey sheet covering your walk. The Ordnance Survey maps are widely available, especially through booksellers and local newsagents.

1

Warton Crags

The path through the old quarry.

Set below a large limestone bluff, there are few villages in the county that have such an august history as Warton. This undulating stroll up and over the rocky spur will reveal the remnants of an Iron Age fort, yet Warton has not only an impressive English history but also an American connection in the shape of the Washington family. A branch of the Washington family came here from Northumberland in the 14th century and on Main Street you can find Washington House, which although rebuilt in the 18th century has a date stone indicating 1612. In 1483 Robert Washington's will provided funds to restore the Norman church. His coat of arms was of a simple stars and stripes design, a pattern which is now world-famous, and the American government ensures that the Stars and Stripes flag still flies proudly on top of the church. One of the Washingtons' daughters married a Spencer and Winston Spencer Churchill could trace his ancestry to this marriage. Fancy that – Churchill and Washington may well have had a blood link! It is also suggested that Lady Diana Spencer could trace her origins back to this area and therefore so can Prince William.

This is a bracing stroll for dogs, with just one potential problem: limestone was once quarried here and what is left are the facing cliffs of the old workings. These are some of the most popular rock climbs and owners need to be aware when climbers are enjoying their sport that the last thing they need is an inquisitive dog. The problem, however, is only at the very start of the walk and only on a few days of the year.

Terrain

A steady climb to Warton Crag, then descending to an undulating green lane.

Where to park

The small car park in Warton village (GR SD498723). **OS map:** OL7 The English Lakes

How to get there

From Carnforth turn off the A6 onto a minor road. Within a couple of miles turn right into Warton village. At a slight incline is the small quarry car park with a much larger car park a little further uphill. The small car park is the starting point for this walk.

Refreshments

Pubs in Warton include the George Washington (☎ 01524 732865) and there are many places to picnic along the way.

The Walk

⦁⦁⦁

⓵ An obvious but very narrow and rocky track leads from the car park to the rock climbing area.

This is a botanist's paradise with limestone flowers and rare butterflies.

Dog factors
⦁⦁⦁

Distance: 2 miles.
Road walking: None.
Livestock: Occasional cattle around point 3
Stiles: 1.
Nearest vets: Alison P. Lee, Carnforth.

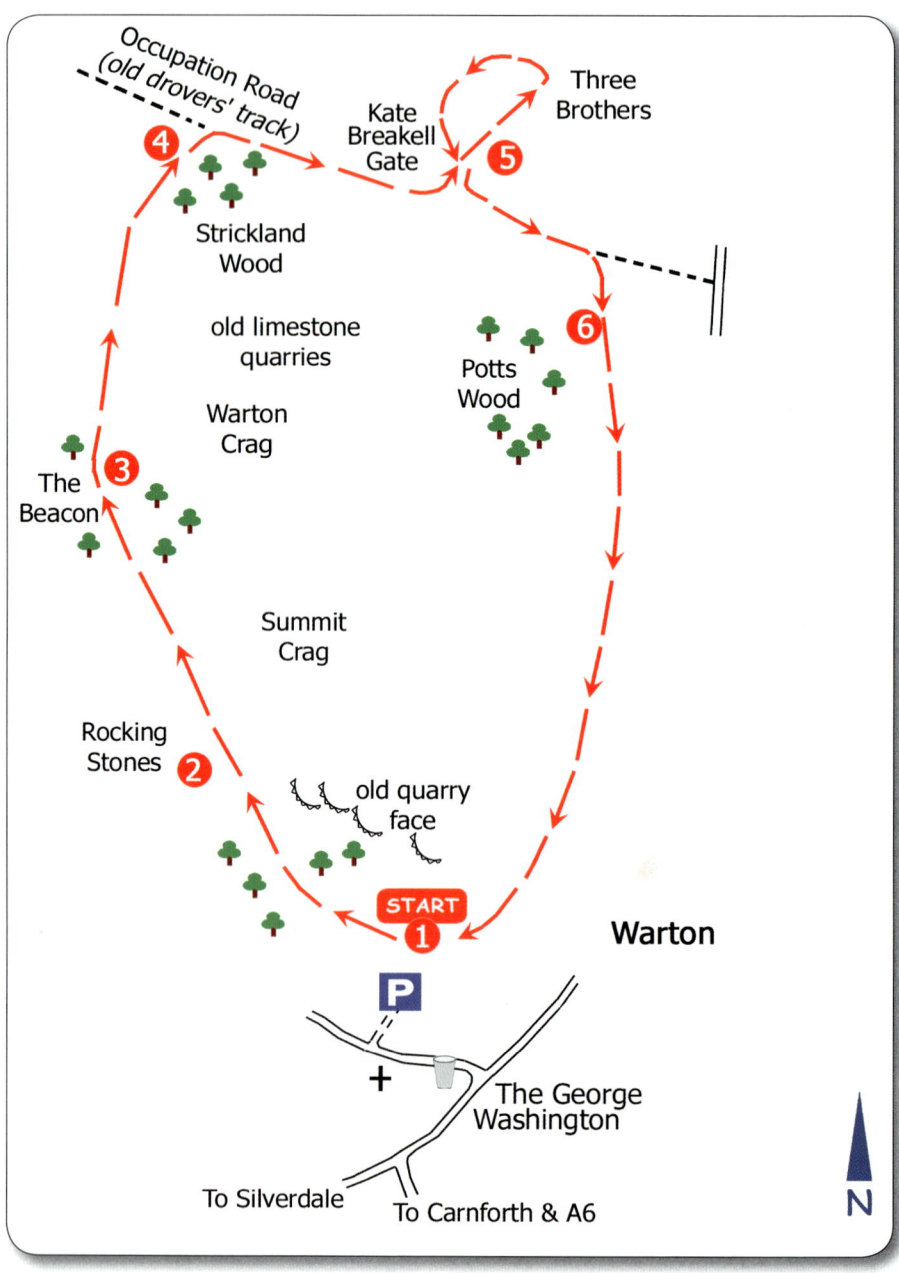

2 The path climbs steadily and below is a restored limekiln. Pass through a gate and the narrow path leads to the **Rocking Stones**, from which there are panoramic views over **Carnforth Marsh**. This leads to **Pinnacle Crag** which presents a challenge for rock climbers.

The Rocking Stones are limestone blocks eroded by centuries of wind and rain. Limestone is composed of the shells of sea creatures which lived in the warm shallow sea that once covered this area.

3 The wooded path, a delight to naturalists and dogs alike, soon reaches the **Beacon**.

This was erected in 1988 to celebrate the bonfire lit in 1588 to warn people of the Spanish Armada, being the start of an invasion designed to rid England of Queen Elizabeth I.

'What's this stick doing across my path?'

This track leads to the flat summit of **Warton Crag** which is 490 ft (150 m) above sea level. During the Iron Age there was an elevated fortification here, where the defenders could command the panoramic views that have changed little over time. Look for a sign to **Crag Foot** and follow a path downhill through trees and then bear right along the **Coach Road** to Warton. There are occasional cattle here during the summer months and their grazing has done much to keep down the rank vegetation and thus improve the habitat.

4 At the back of Warton Crag is reached the **Occupation Road**.

This name is somewhat confusing and I much prefer to call it the Old Drovers Road. In the old days before refrigeration, live cattle were driven from often-distant markets and the drovers had fixed routes and favourite resting places. The dogs who guarded them were known as talbots and they were a cross between a sheep dog and a guard dog.

Turn right along this road and keep a look out for horse riders and mountain bikers. This reaches the **Kate Breakell Gate**.

5 Through another gate on the left is a path to the **Three Brothers**, a circular diversion along a permissive footpath and well worth a visit.

This splendid trio of rocks are the sort known as erratics and are stones of a geological type not known to the area. They were brought from the Lake District by retreating glaciers some 10,000 years ago and now stand in splendid isolation above the limestone blocks.

After returning to the **Occupation Road** follow the undulating path described by some as a green lane, which indeed it is.

6 Pass **Potts Wood** and the sign for a local nature reserve. This is also worth a short diversion. The obvious track leads back to the starting point at the car park.

2

Hest Bank and Bolton-le-Sands

Setting off along the salt marshes.

This walk has long been a favourite of mine because I enjoy strolling and birdwatching. This is why I have lived so long with an assortment of Labradors: they have that gun dog instinct to be inquisitive and yet obedient. The start is perfect at low water with the birdlife visible at a distance and with lots of splash pools left over from the last tide to stimulate dogs. The views over Morecambe Bay are at all times spectacular. It is wise to invest in a set of tide tables and to time your walk to be at its best. This is not because of danger but to allow your pet to roam at will among the marshes. At high tide this RSPB site is a great place to watch wildfowl and waders, especially in the colder months of the year. Dogs and serious birdwatchers do not mix but apart from at 'peak bird times' there is no problem. This is one of the very best places for dog owners to meet and discuss canine matters.

The walk links two historic settlements, each with its own history and character. Hest Bank is coastal and popular with those in search of views of

Morecambe Bay, whilst Bolton-le-Sands was on the old coach road and is also split by the Lancaster Canal. Bolton-le-Sands did not develop a direct railway link and the village we see today is in a delightful time warp relating to the days of coach and horses and the canal. The hostelry called the Ship has a somewhat misleading name because it catered for the canal-based barges rather than sailing ships. This stretch of the canal is ideal for dogs, as well as those interested in birdlife.

Terrain

Canal towpath and flat marshland.

Where to park

There are lots of parking areas on the shoreline (GR SD468667). **OS map:** OL41 Forest of Bowland & Ribblesdale.

How to get there

On the A6 from Carnforth to Lancaster, look out for traffic lights. Turn right and follow the A5105 towards Morecambe to reach Hest Bank. Turn right to the railway and negotiate the level crossing controlled by traffic lights and barrier to arrive at the shoreline.

Refreshments

There is no shortage here with pubs and cafés all around, including a very popular fish and chip shop. Dog lovers will find a warm welcome at the Shore Café in season which carries a notice 'Dogs Welcome. Owners tolerated'. Here are bowls of water, and there are picnic tables close to the railway.

The Walk

. . . .

1 Pass a small caravan park to the right and follow the shoreline.

2 Walk along a grassy footpath between pleasant houses and allow your dog to

Dog factors

. . . .

Distance: 4½ miles.
Road walking: About ½ mile.
Livestock: None.
Stiles: 4.
Nearest vets: Bay Veterinary Centre, Morecambe.

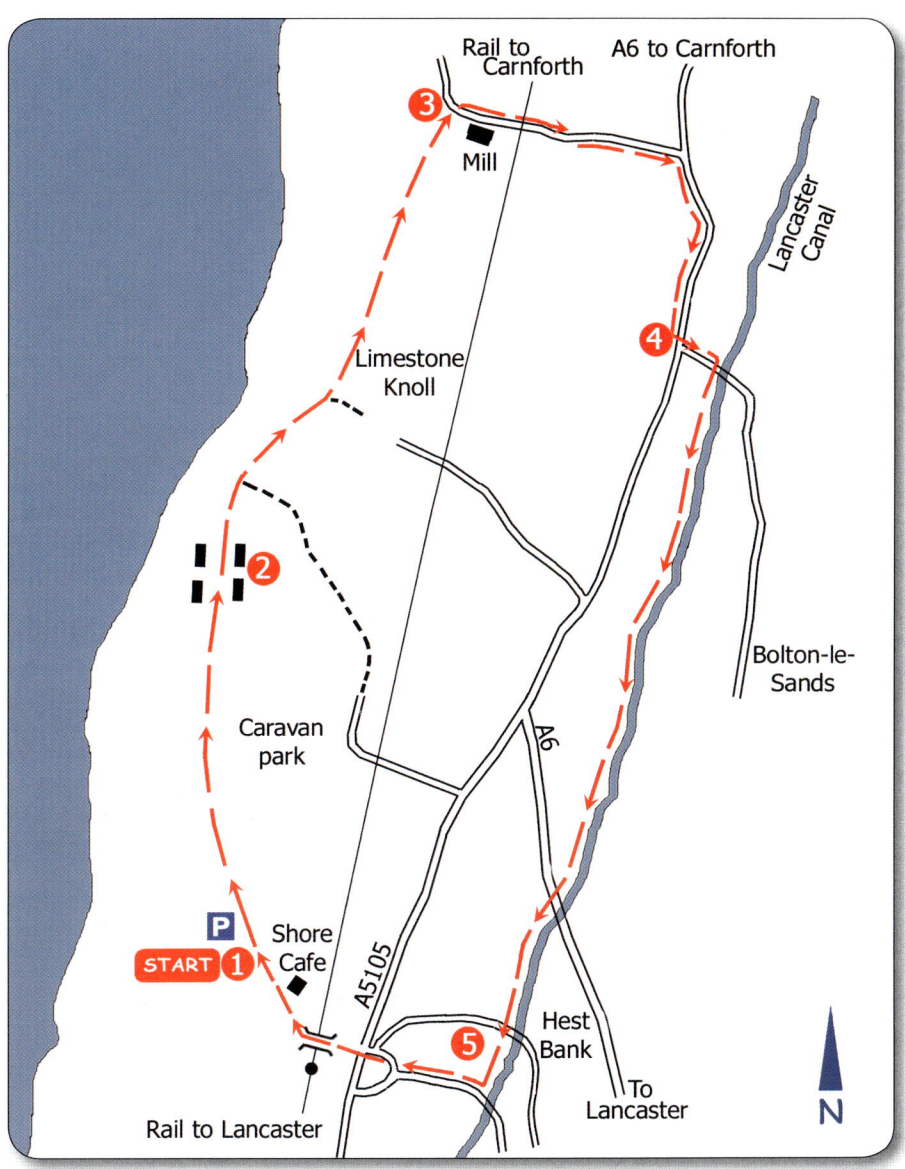

Rail to Carnforth

A6 to Carnforth

③

Mill

Lancaster Canal

Limestone Knoll

④

Bolton-le-Sands

②

Caravan park

A6

P

Shore Cafe

START ①

A5105

Hest Bank

⑤

To Lancaster

Rail to Lancaster

N

roam around the salt marshes to the left. Pass a limestone knoll on the right which has lots of ledges ideal for picnics.

This is covered in trees and ferns which are of great interest all through the year. For dogs it is a never-ending source of sticks and scents.

3 Approach the building which is a long disused mill close to a very minor road. Turn right and pass under the railway to reach the A6. Turn right along the footpath alongside this road which is very busy. Obviously care is needed here. It is only a short stretch of road but dogs need to be kept under close control.

4 Cross the road and look out for a set of steps leading onto the **Lancaster Canal**. Turn right along the towpath.

Work began on this initially lockless canal linking Preston with Kendal in 1796 but this section was only finally opened to traffic in 1819. At this time it was of vital importance because it allowed cheap coal to be brought in from Lancashire to power the industries around Carnforth and Lancaster. The boom days were short-lived however because by the 1850s the railways were dominating the transport system.

5 Follow the towpath until you reach a set of stone steps indicating **Hest Bank**. Dogs should be on a lead at this point. Descend the steps to reach the railway, the level crossing and the starting point on the shore. This walk should satisfy most dogs but those with any energy left can have another romp on the salt marshes at the conclusion of the stroll.

The welcoming Shore Café near the start of the walk.

3

Stocks Reservoir

Stocks reservoir dam.

From the very start of this walk there are panoramic views over the reservoir and a noticeboard illustrates the work of the Bowland Initiative, which is a joint venture by the water company United Utilities and the RSPB. This involves managing the whole area for the benefit of wildlife, including the forest and the nearby heather moors. On this walk dog lovers need not worry and they can relax and enjoy birdwatching whilst their pooch can have a good root around and maybe a mud bath in wet weather. This route can be enjoyed at any time of the year and birdwatchers can look out for the increasingly common buzzards and the very rare hen harrier. In winter the wildfowl watches are always interesting and at times can be spectacular. Here are large flocks of Canada geese plus whooper swans, pochard, tufted duck, goosander and teal plus many other species.

Lancashire – A Dog Walker's Guide

Terrain

This is the longest walk in this book but the terrain is easy and well within the capabilities of most canines. Because this is a long walk I always take water for the dog. Inka drinks directly from a bottle but just in case I always carry a fold-up plastic dog bowl.

Where to park

The free car park at Gisburn Forest (GR SD732565). **OS map:** 103 Blackburn & Burnley, or OL41 Forest of Bowland & Ribblesdale.

How to get there

From Long Preston take the B6478 through Wigglesworth and Tosside. Follow the road towards Slaidburn to reach a narrow minor road to the right. Take this and pass Dalehead church on the right and the reservoir on the left. The car park of Gisburn Forest will then be seen to the left.

Refreshments

There is an excellent picnic site close to the reservoir and pubs in the area include the Plough Inn at Wigglesworth, ☎ 01729 840243.

Dog factors

Distance: 7 miles – allow 3 hours.
Road walking: Minimal, about ½ mile.
Livestock: Sheep may be encountered at point 3.
Stiles: 3, but all easy to negotiate.
Nearest vets: Mearley Veterinary Group, Clitheroe.

The Walk

1 From the car park follow the obvious track, around which are information boards describing the history of the reservoir and the village which was flooded to supply water to the Fylde coast. There is another notice-board indicating three woodland walks which are colour coded according to difficulty (each of which is dog-friendly), but this walk ignores these trails and passes a picnic site to the right.

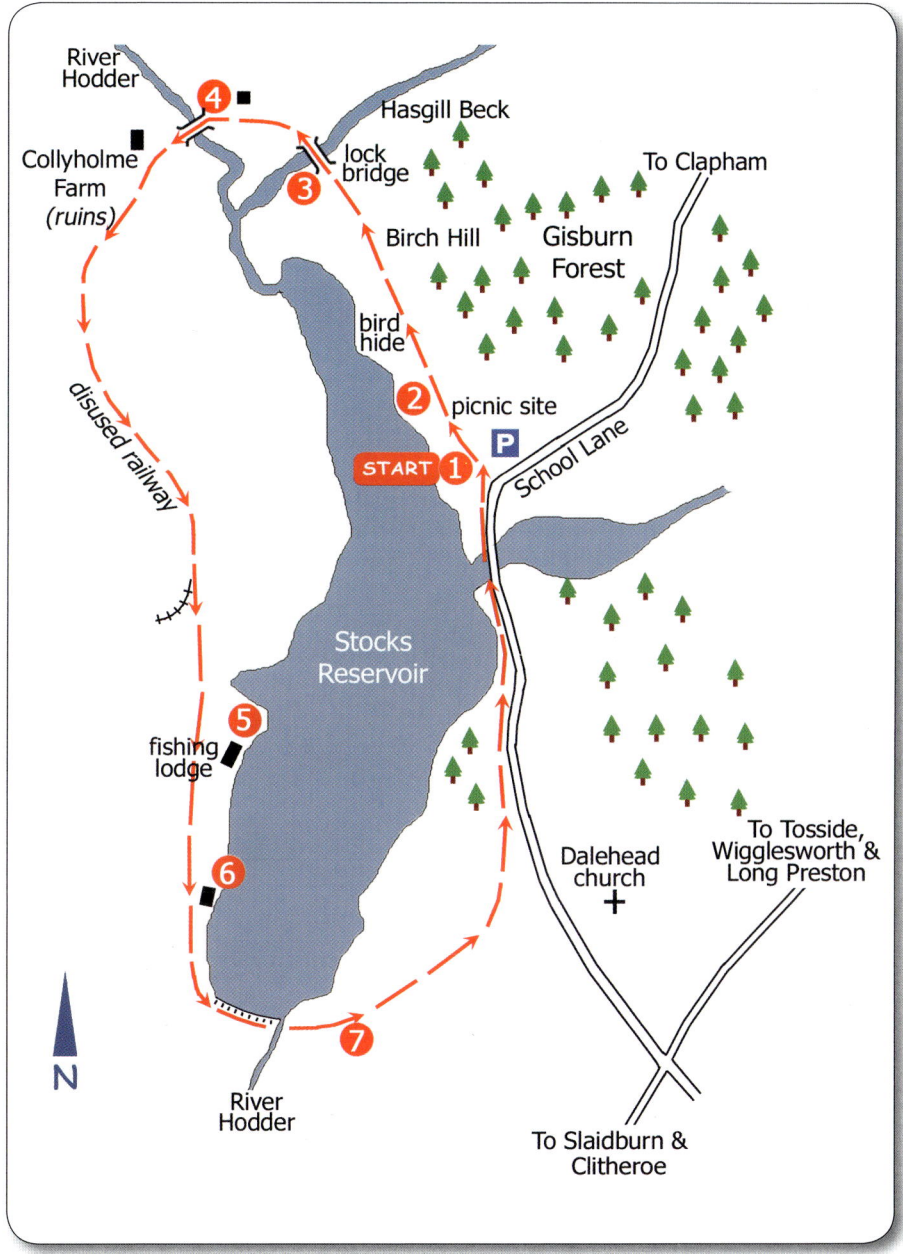

Lancashire – A Dog Walker's Guide

This impressive house is now used by United Utilities.

Stocks Reservoir opened in 1932 and is one of the largest in the north of England. It has a maximum depth of 100 ft (32 m) and a capacity of 3,059 million gallons (12 billion litres). During the 1960s the Forestry Commission planted up the mainly coniferous Gisburn Forest and this is now an area where dogs can roam free and absorb every scent, and there is no shortage of twigs to chase. The walk takes you around the reservoir on a route of woodland and water.

2 Continue along the obvious track, but perhaps divert for a short distance to the left to reach a very impressive bird hide.

I always look to ensure that the hide is not occupied before letting Inka in. Inside is a notebook full of bird sightings in which visitors are asked to make their contribution.

Return to the track and ascend gently up to **Birch Hill**.

As its name implies this is an area dominated by silver and common birch and a real contrast to the mainly dominant conifer forest. There was once a farm here but all that now remains are a few stones which were the footings.

3 Approach **Lock Bridge** which spans **Hasgill Beck**. Cross the bridge and follow the old trackway which once linked Birch Hill Farm with other farms at Hasgill and New House. Both the New House Farm and barn are now derelict but the land is still farmed and owners need to have dogs under control if sheep are in the area.

4 Bear left to reach and cross a footbridge over the **River Hodder** as it flows towards Stocks Reservoir and is absorbed by it. After this, look out for the ruins of **Collyholme Farm**.

Here also can be seen the old railway track which was once vital to supply raw materials needed during the construction of the reservoir. The route follows this old track, though only parts of it can now be recognised as such.

5 The track passes **Hollins** (meaning holly) to reach the fishing lodge.

At the fisherman's hut, permits to fish are available during the season and refreshments are often available. There are also places to picnic.

6 Carry on to pass the **Stocks Reservoir Board Office**, an impressive building that looks like a Tudor manor house – it is hard to imagine that it was only completed around the 1930s. Now approach Stocks reservoir dam and enjoy the sight and sound of the massive overflow as water is released to provide a supply to the River Hodder.

7 At the end of the dam, cross a stile and join yet another section of the old railway track. Follow this through a woodland area to reach the road, almost opposite the church.

8 Pass through another substantial stile and keep left across the causeway between the main reservoir and a pond. Cross another stile and return to the car park.

4

Slaidburn and Croasdale Brook

The River Hodder.

It is hard to rival such a lovely river walk as this, through beautiful and historic countryside and alongside a literally babbling brook. Croasdale Brook is a tributary of the River Hodder and flows through the lower part of Slaidburn, overlooked by a splendid village green. Until the boundary changes of 1974 Slaidburn was in Yorkshire but Lancashire has welcomed the area with open arms. Since Norman times it has been regarded as the focal point of the Forest of Bowland and the whole region is now classified as an Area of Outstanding Natural Beauty.

Those interested in the history of the village will find a warm greeting from the volunteers in the heritage centre. Look out for the Old Grammar School built in 1717 which is now part of the village junior school. In the church of St Andrew, dating mainly from the 15th century a set of dog tongs is on display, used in the days when parishioners travelled a long way to church and brought their animals with them for protection. These tongs and a whip were used to keep badly-behaved canines in order!

Terrain

This stroll is a quiet and usually sparsely-populated riverside ramble.

Where to park

The walk begins by the Hark to Bounty pub in Slaidburn. There is plenty of free and pay and display parking in the village. Excellent toilet facilities at the village car park (GR SD714523). **OS map:** OL41 Forest of Bowland & Ribblesdale

How to get there

From Clitheroe follow the narrow twisting B6478 through the attractive villages of Waddington and Newton to Slaidburn.

Refreshments

This is a village very popular with tourists and there is no shortage of good places to eat. The Hark to Bounty pub once held the Forest of Bowland court and in a room upstairs the old judicial furniture has been retained and puts a whole new meaning to the phrase 'Called to the Bar'. The pub caters for well-behaved dogs. ☎ 01200 446246.

The Walk

. . . .

❶ From the **Hark to Bounty** pub, ignore the minor road alongside the pub and follow the main road through the village. On the ascent just after the Health

Dog factors

. . . .

Distance: 4 miles.
Road walking: Very minimal.
Livestock: Seldom a problem, but sheep can be present towards the end of the walk.
Stiles: 11 simple and easy to negotiate; 1 hurdle stile over which heavy and older dogs may need help; 1 ladder stile which is more easily negotiated.
Nearest vets: Mearley Veterinary Group, Clitheroe.

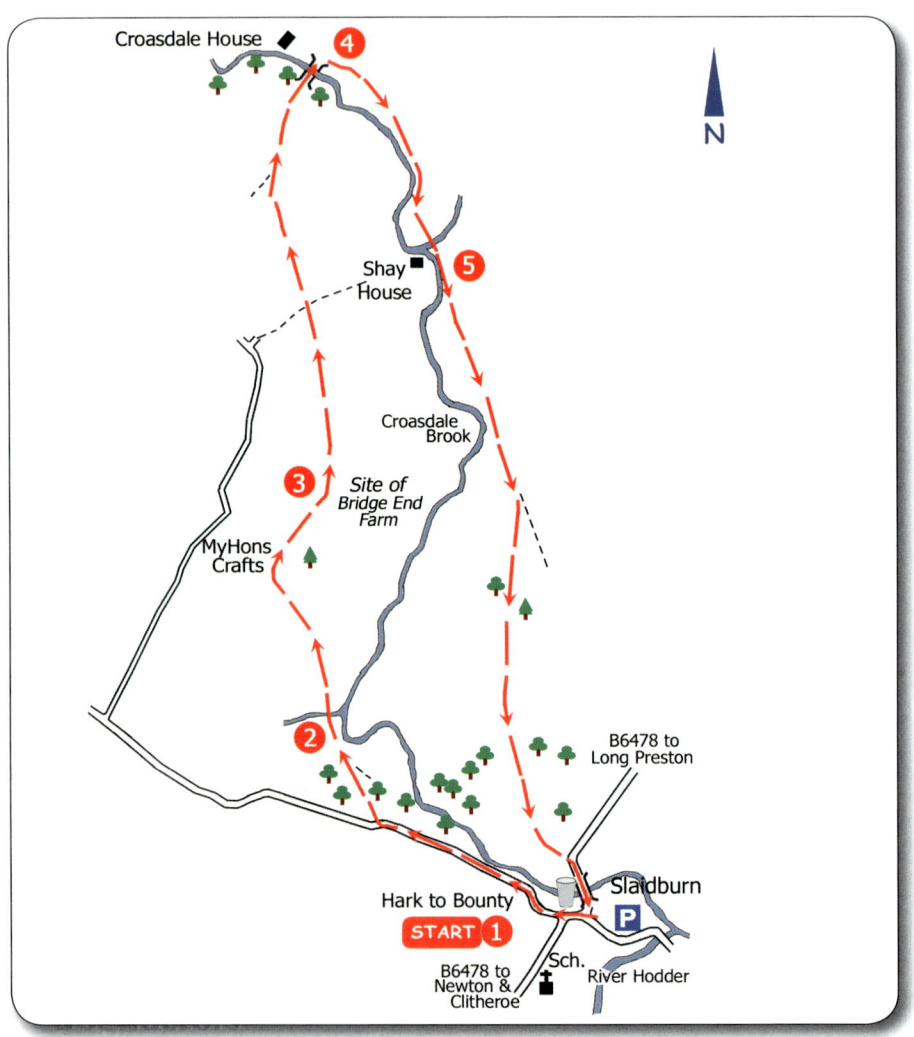

Centre look out for an obvious path to the right. This leads into a splendid little woodland full of doggie smells and the chance to chase loose sticks. Here also are the rippling waters of Croasdale Brook. At the end of the belt of trees is an easy-to-negotiate stile.

2 Follow the brook for a short distance and then ascend to the left to reach another stile in a field with a surrounding hedge. After a wall stile, pass over a slab bridge crossing a small stream and bear right towards **Myttons Farm Crafts**. Cross the driveway of **Wood House**.

③ Bear right and cross over to reach a corner stile. Go across another little bridge to reach the now derelict **Bridge End Farm** which must once have been an impressive structure. There are panoramic views ahead to Croasdale Fell, which is the main catchment area for the brook. At the end of the field, go right to cross a contoured field close to **Simfield House**. Pass over a hurdle stile, which is not as difficult for dogs to negotiate as its name implies but aged canines may need a little persuasion. From a small footbridge the route negotiates a wooded area to reach a kissing gate.

④ On reaching a wooden footbridge over the main **Croasdale Brook** pass over this and turn right. For the rest of this walk the watercourse is still on the right but now the flow is back towards Slaidburn. Take time here to explore a weir and a small but attractive waterfall. Continue downstream to reach the area of **Shay House** farm.

⑤ On reaching the drive to this property do not enter but look for a stile opposite and continue to follow the line of the brook. At this point the route bears away to the left of the meander of the brook and at a wall, negotiate another ladder stile. Ease gently towards the brook to find a wall stile in the corner. Then negotiate a series of easy to cross stiles and follow the undulations, with super views behind of the Croasdale upland. Approach a line of trees and to the left you will see a corner stile. Pass through this and descend into **Slaidburn**, reaching a bridge over the **River Hodder.** Turn right back to the starting point or left to the village car park.

St Andrew's church, Slaidburn.

5

Gisburn

One of the crenellated bridges on the Gisburn estate.

Here is a delightful route that treks gently through Gisburne Park, with its supposed connection with Guy of Gisburne who was such a thorn in the flesh of Robin Hood. The old name for the settlement had an 'e' on the end but this was left off when the railway timetables were drawn up and so the name became Gisburn. The walk then carries on via quaint bridges over Stock Beck, a substantial watercourse that is a tributary of the River Ribble, before returning to Gisburn village.

At one time Gisburn was an important staging post on the turnpike route between Clitheroe and Skipton but only one of these old pubs – the White Bull

– remains open to this day. Another of the old hostelries is Cromwell House, dating to 1635. Now a private house, it was once called the Ribblesdale Arms and had a famous resident ghost.

After a stretch of roadside walking dogs will love this stile-free walk with lots of fields, trees and water – a pooches' paradise.

Dog factors

Distance: 4 miles.
Road walking: 1 mile along a quiet road, plus a short section of the A59.
Livestock: Very occasional.
Stiles: None.
Nearest vets: Mearley Veterinary Group, Clitheroe.

Terrain
Woodland and river paths, with a stretch through open parkland.

Where to park
On Mill Lane close to the cattle and sheep auction mart. The walk starts from the village church (GR SD830488). **OS map:** OL21 South Pennines or OL41 Forest of Bowland & Ribblesdale.

How to get there
Gisburn lies astride the busy A59 between Clitheroe and Skipton.

Refreshments
The Fountain Inn in Barnoldswick (☎ 01282 813412) serves food every lunchtime. Dogs are welcome in the bar area and there is a small seated yard outside.

The Walk

1 Start from the recently restored parish church of **St Mary the Virgin**.

The church has a Norman tower plus some stonework in the nave taken from Sawley Abbey after its Dissolution in 1537. Inside are memorials to the Lister family

Lancashire – A Dog Walker's Guide

who later became Lords Ribblesdale and whose home was in Gisburne Park. In the churchyard look out for the grave of Francis Duckworth. He was a famous composer of hymns during the early 20th century. His tunes were named after local villages, the most famous being Rimington, which is close to Gisburn and the place where Duckworth was born.

From the church follow the A59 to reach the slip road off to the right, signed 'Bolton-by-Bowland'. The livestock auction mart is on the left and further on are buildings associated with the old station. Sadly this is no longer in use but the railway line is still open and connects Blackburn with Hellifield. Follow the road towards Bolton-by-Bowland and descend through mature woodland.

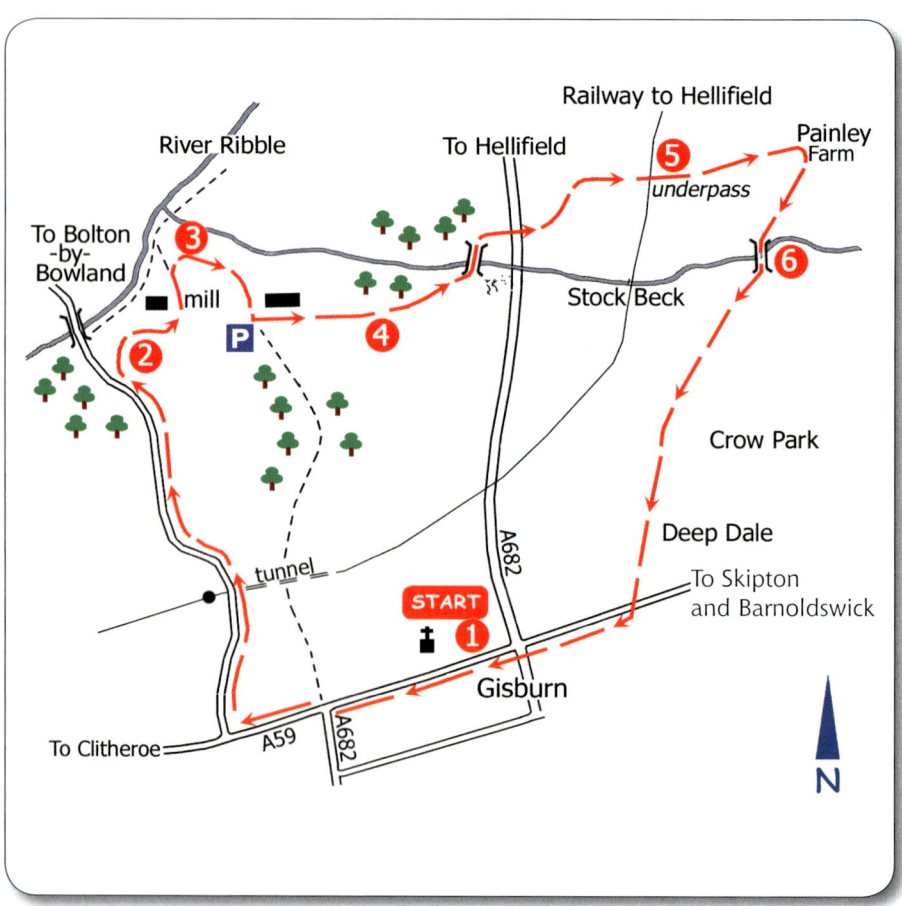

2 Approach **Gisburn Bridge** spanning the **River Ribble** but do not cross this. Bear right through the grounds of a private dwelling which was once an old mill. Look out for inscribed stones taken from the ruins of Sawley Abbey.

This stretch of the Ribble was once an important haunt of otters but in the 1970s a combination of chemical pollution and hunting with hounds had brought the species close to extinction. With the strength of the Wildlife and Countryside Act behind it the otter has returned and is one of the few wild mammals which can more than match a keen Labrador in swimming strength. Both animals use their tails as a powerful rudder.

Follow a wide track and then turn right.

The approach to Gisburn bridge.

Lancashire – A Dog Walker's Guide

3 You are now entering the doggie paradise called **Gisburne Park**. Pass **Gisburne Park Private Hospital** on the left, housed in what was once the home of Lord Ribblesdale.

This splendid building dates to 1750 but there was a Lister residence long before this time. The first of the family to be created Lord Ribblesdale should be remembered for his planting of a million oak trees, many of which still grace the area much to the delight of human and canine visitors alike.

A wide track leads back to the village but our route carries on into the woodland.

4 Continue through the trees to reach a delightful little bridge over Stock Beck which is a substantial tributary of the River Ribble. Ascend a wooded bank to reach the A682 to Hellifield. Cross this road carefully and pass through a gate opposite. The track heads across a field through which runs a tiny stream and then goes through an underpass beneath the railway.

In the 1850s the Listers were not pleased that the railway was pushing through their estate but they were offered substantial compensation. A further compromise was reached, with all bridges through Gisburn Park being built to resemble small medieval castles!

5 As the obvious track meanders through fields and gates look south to see the whale-like hump of Pendle Hill and the foothills of Weets Hill. The **Painley** farm complex is a real reminder of old England with lots of old barns. Continue walking through this generous slice of agricultural history before bearing right to descend to **Stock Beck**.

6 Cross a footbridge and enjoy the stream itself – especially if you are a canine paddler – and then ascend a grassy bank to **Crow Park**. Pass through a farmyard area (dogs on leads here, please) to reach the A59 east of **Gisburn**. Turn right to return to the church.

Knott End

Bono beachcombing at Knott End.

It is its isolation that gives Knott End its attraction for modern-day visitors, especially as it is bordered on two sides by the sea and the river. The present car park is on the site of the old railway station, the line once linking to the main line and which was built with the intention of developing a major seaside resort but this did not materialise. The walk follows the shoreline before turning inland where there is splendid countryside and an added bonus of a haunted manor house. Some dogs I know love to travel on the passenger ferry across to Fleetwood, which can be caught close to the start and finish of the walk.

Parts of this walk are close to the estuary area and when the tide is in there are plenty of opportunities for dogs to swim. Because the area is salty, be sure to include plenty of water for your dog at the end of the walk. The strand line is full of fascinating objects including sticks and irresistible strands of rope which my Labradors have never been able to resist.

Lancashire – A Dog Walker's Guide

Terrain

Easy shoreline walking, with woodland paths and brief inclines.

Where to park

There is a pay and display car park at Knott End, within reach of the passenger ferry to Fleetwood across the Wyre estuary (GR SD347486). **OS map:** Landranger 102 Preston & Blackpool.

How to get there

Knott End is a cul-de-sac at the terminus of the B5270. It is 1 mile from Preesall village which is clearly signed from the A588 Lancaster to Fleetwood road.

Nearest refreshments

There are a couple of good small cafés on the main road leading to the ferry or why not take a picnic?

The Walk

● ●

1 From the car park at Knott End and close to the coastguard station, head in the direction of the old **Bourne Arms Hotel**. Follow the paved esplanade and approach the village shops but head towards the viewpoint plinth. Follow a good track running parallel with the solid sea defences, which were strengthened during the Second World War and again in recent times. From a group of houses and caravan parks at the well-named **Sandy Bay** look for a prominent set of concrete steps to the right.

2 Move away from the shore by descending the steps, and put the dog on the lead to pass through the caravan park to a residential lane. Cross the lane and look to the left. Join a signed footpath, cross a line of stiles and go over two footbridges to reach a farm track.

Dog factors

● ●

Distance: 5 miles.
Road walking: Some, but there are lots of dog-friendly areas as well.
Livestock: None.
Stiles: 7 but only one is not easy to negotiate.
Nearest vets: The Mount Veterinary Centre, Fleetwood.

3 Turn right along this track and follow it as it winds between buildings, where it is best to keep dogs on leads but don't worry as there are plenty of exercise areas to come. The track veers right into **Little Tongues Lane**. At the junction with the main road turn left and follow the road for about 200 yards and at a bus stop look for a stile.

4 Cross the stile and take the obvious field path, over a set of easy-to-negotiate stiles to reach a footbridge at the bottom of a steep incline. The route then climbs towards another stile immediately in front of **Preesall junior school**.

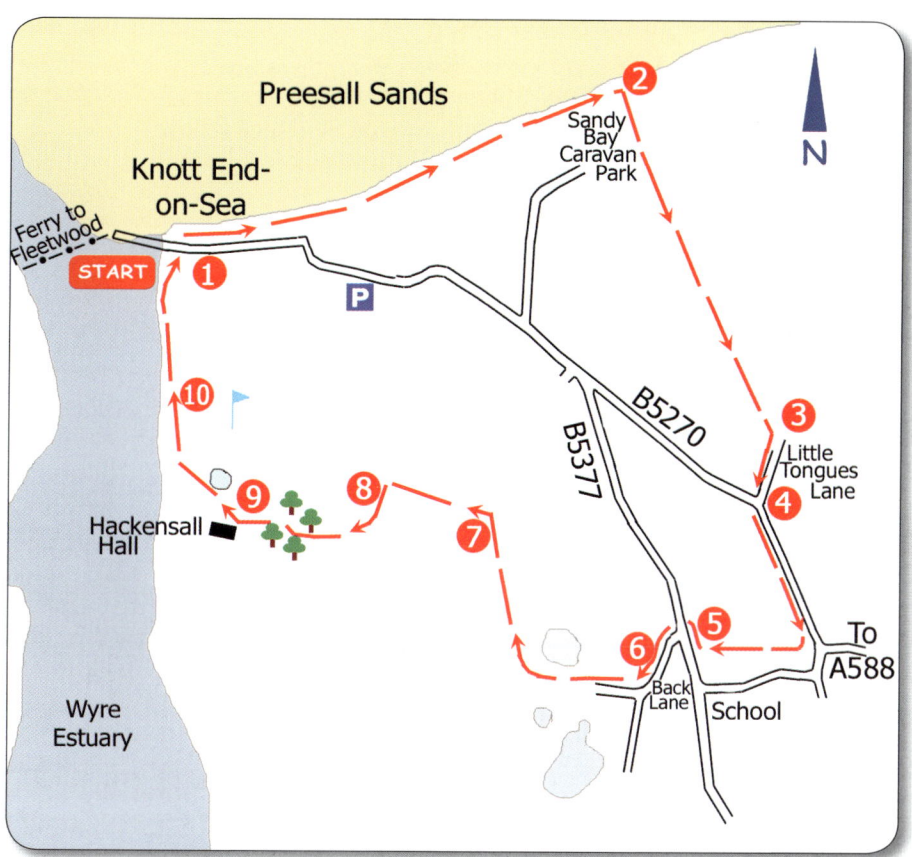

5 Turn right at this point and follow an enclosed footpath isolating the school and then turn right at the entrance. Continue ahead to join a narrow lane winding to the right towards the village. Pass through a complex of buildings leading to the main road.

This was once an industrial area dominated by salt mines, the major employer in the area. Salt was exported by boat but a pipeline was built across the Wyre to the ICI factory at Thornton on the opposite bank. Brine was pumped along this pipe to the factory.

6 Cross over to **Back Lane** and continue along this to the right. This now becomes **Acres Lane**. Turn right along the lane and this narrows into a dog-friendly path. Pass a fishing pond and a junction of three footpaths. Follow the one signed **Curwens Hill**. Ascend this path towards farm buildings but before you reach these go over a wall stile and turn right. Cross a field and follow the edge close to a line of trees and descend to reach a kissing gate in the corner.

7 Turn left at the kissing gate and follow the line of the disused railway.

This was planned as the Knott End to Garstang railway, which was better known as the 'Pilling Pig' because of the squealing sound made by the steam engines. This opened in 1908 as a service for local farmers and only closed in 1950. One of the locomotives has been preserved and is on display at the entrance of a nearby caravan park at Pilling.

Follow this obvious track towards a small area of woodland. Pass beneath the trees leading to three paths. Take the middle route.

8 At the end of this path, turn sharp left towards a farmhouse then bear right into woodland and ignore less obvious tracks leading to the right and left. Follow a signpost indicating 'Knott End ¾ mile' and pass **Hackensall Hall**.

This 17th-century manor house was built on the site of a much earlier dwelling and the site is said to be haunted.

9 Look out for another signpost. Turn right and follow the **Wyre Way** and pass alongside a prominent hedge. Cross the golf links, keeping dogs on a lead and keep a wary eye open for badly driven golf balls. At a wooden building turn

Looking towards the Wyre Estuary.

right and follow a very obvious track between shore cliffs and the golf course. Here dogs can romp close to the sea and follow the sea wall.

10 Turn right and follow the sea wall back to the car park. With the tide in, there is a chance for yet another canine dip but don't forget that drink of water at the end of this energetic and exciting stroll. This drink is important because the walk is close to the sea and debris is coated with salt.

Greenberfield Locks and Barnoldswick

The Leeds and Liverpool canal at Greenberfield Locks.

Strolls including a stretch of canal are a joy because colourful pleasure craft are often on the move and boaters are friendly folk. Many have dogs, which take to canal life rather like ducks to water. To the canal enthusiast the Greenberfield area is full of interest because here the Leeds and Liverpool canal starts its long descent into Yorkshire. There is a fascinating section on the walk showing that not all canal construction went smoothly. By 1820 it had been realised that the existing line of locks was using far too much water. A new line had to be cut and a bridge, a lock house and a former stretch of canal were left literally dry. Despite the passage of almost 200 years the old line is still clearly visible whilst the new line of locks is kept busy as pleasure barges pass through.

This walk has an additional treasure as it passes one of the most historic little churches in Britain – St Mary-le-Ghyll. In 1147 twelve monks from Fountains Abbey set out to establish a daughter house and settled on land on which now stands Barnoldswick. This area already had an important parish church at nearby Bracewell and the locals did not welcome the new monks. This, coupled with a series of harsh winters, made them decide to relocate and they eventually settled at Kirkstall. The land remained in the abbey's hands, however, and here at Ghyll is a reminder of monastic ambitions in Barnoldswick. St Mary-le-Ghyll is a lovely building still in a splendid state of repair. Inside there is a three-decker pulpit and a fine set of box pews. Sadly these days the church is kept locked but those who wish to go inside should telephone 01282 812028.

Terrain

A dog's paradise with a long stretch of canal towpath, a leafy lane and a footpath down through fields and close to a pretty little stream.

Where to park

The free car park at Greenberfield Locks (GR SD888482). **OS map:** OL41 Forest of Bowland & Ribblesdale.

How to get there

From the centre of Barnoldswick, take a minor road (the B6252) towards Thornton-in-Craven. About 2 miles beyond Barnoldswick, take the left turn to Greenberfield Locks. Descend the narrow, twisting road to the car park on the left.

Nearest refreshments

The Lock Stop café near the car park has picnic tables outside where dogs are welcome.

Dog factors
· ·
Distance: 4 miles.
Road walking: Just over ½ mile.
Livestock: None.
Stiles: None.
Nearest vets: Stanley House Veterinary Surgeons, Barnoldswick.

The Walk

1 From the café and heading away from the locks, pass the water inlet on the right. Look out for a line of seats and pass under **bridge No 156** (and bear in mind that bridge No 155 does not now exist). Look to the right of the towpath to find a canal milestone which reads 'Liverpool 86 miles, Leeds 41¼ miles'. Approach the Rolls-Royce factory and then reach **bridge No 154A** located at a sharp bend in the canal.

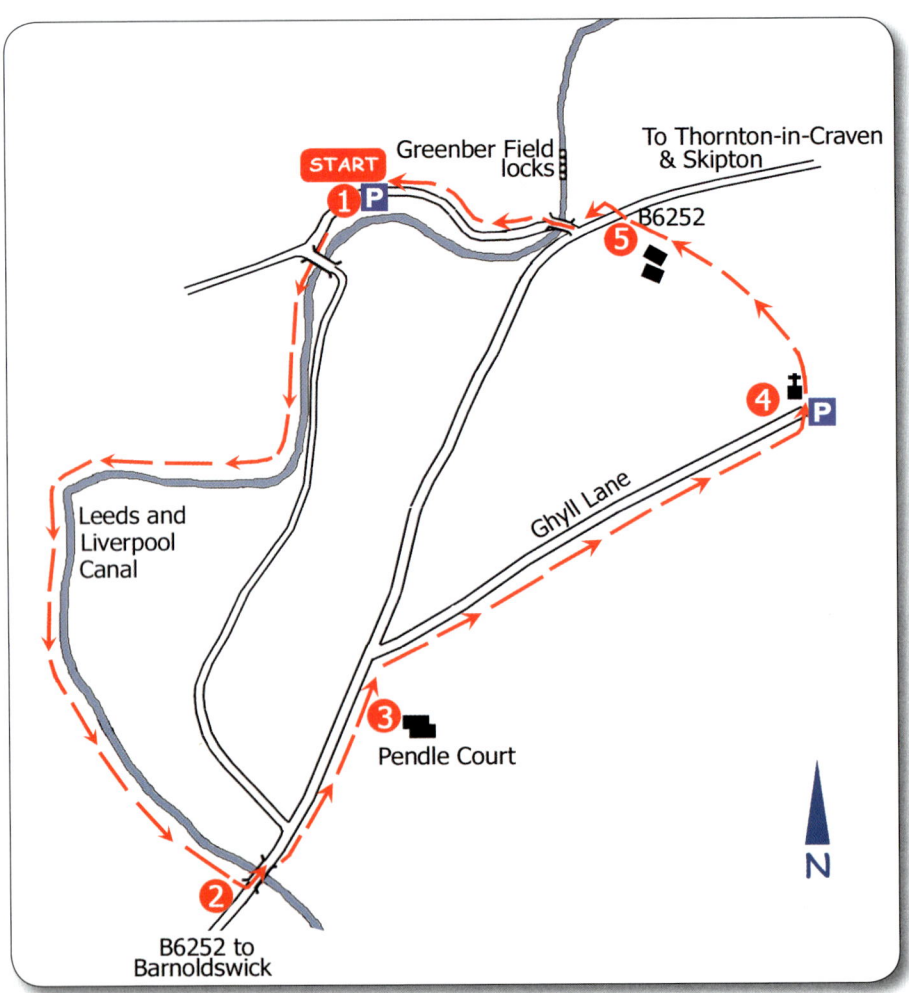

2 Pass under the bridge and turn right to ascend a set of stone steps to reach the road. For the next ½ mile your dog should be on the lead along the road. There is a lot more freedom to come! Turn right along the road and pass **Pendle Court** on the right.

3 Carry on and follow the wide grassy footpath and soon find **Ghyll Lane** on the right. Cross the road and turn left to follow the pleasant dog-friendly track to reach **St Mary-le-Ghyll church**. Along this track are little lay-bys full of fascinating scents.

'Are we going on board?'

The church is in a splendid state of repair. The roof is a classic example of 13th-century architecture and the tower dates to 1524, all paid for by the monks based at Kirkstall. There is a Latin inscription on the tower which seems to suggest a date of '524' but the mason missed out the M which in Latin means one thousand. The monks deliberately built this church in a remote place in order to keep well away from the local people who were not very welcoming.

4 From the rear of the church – still used and surrounded by a large graveyard – descend along a very pleasant footpath through fields and farms and alongside a pretty stream. Here is an ideal place for dogs to splash and swim. Continue to descend to reach the B6252. Cross over this road.

5 Close by is a brown sign leading to **Greenberfield Lane**. Follow this twisting route with views down to the two lines of canal – one wet and one dry – and in around ¼ mile return to the car park.

Calder Vale

The old mill buildings at Calder Vale.

Calder Vale was a creditable attempt to create a model village showing how a textile mill community should be organised. This, in 1835, was the ambition of the Quaker brothers, Richard and Jonathan Jackson. They chose an area of the River Calder, a small tributary of the River Wyre, set in a wooded valley. In time two mills were built including Low Mill and the four-storeyed Lappet Mill which still works 24 hours a day and produces red, black and white chequered cloth exported to Arab countries and used as head wear. The walk follows the river out of the hamlet, where it is the haunt of grey wagtail, pied wagtail and dippers, with all three species being resident. There are good canine paddling areas here, and there are trees in the valley leading to one of the best displays of springtime bluebells to be seen anywhere in Lancashire. The waving sea of blue in this area contrasts sharply with the white star-like flowers of ramsons, also known as stinking onions or wild garlic. Most of my dogs have been unable to resist having a good chew at the leaves of this plant. At the high point of the walk there are views over to Blackpool Tower on a fine day.

Human visitors will be pleased that so much of this historic village has survived and their canine companions should be glad that much of the wooded valley dating back many centuries has also survived.

Dog factors

Distance: 2 miles.
Road walking: All track and road .
Livestock: Little, if any.
Stiles: None, but there are cattle grids, with gates at the side.
Nearest vets: Arcade Veterinary Centre, Garstang.

Terrain

There are a few rocky areas and inclines but these are all easily negotiated.

Where to park

There is a large car park close to the mill which is the starting point of the walk (GR SD533458). **OS map:** OL41 Forest of Bowland & Ribblesdale.

How to get there

Calder Vale is set in a valley and is reached via a cul-de-sac. From the A6 at Garstang, follow the Beacon Fell signs. Then go over the Lancaster Canal and pass the Kenlis Arms. Go along Sandholme Lane and Strickens Lane to reach Calder Vale and the mill. The mill is still busy and so this walk is at its best at the weekend and evenings.

Refreshments

None all the year round but local ladies often organise splendid bluebell teas during this 'blooming season' and these events should not be missed.

The Walk

1 From the old police station and post office, cross the little bridge over the **River Calder**.

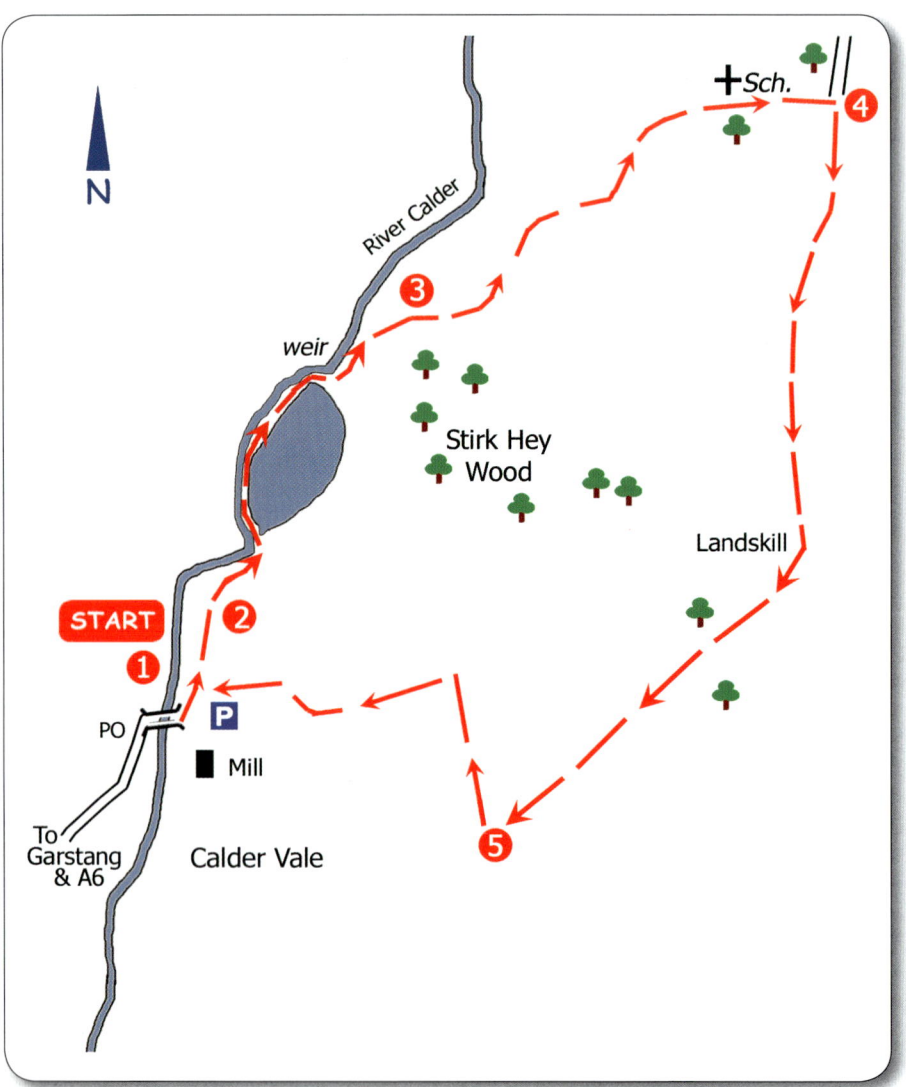

There are many fast-moving tributary streams here which were obviously ideal for powering small and very early textile mills.

Follow the quiet road to the left and pass the long row of mill workers' cottages.

② At the end of the cottages go through a gate, follow the tarmac track along the river and negotiate a steep but steady incline. Look out for the weir on the river, which was obviously built to accelerate the flow of water to the mills.

③ Continue through the woodland with lots of clearings for dogs to explore, to arrive at a gate leading to the school and church.

The Brock Valley picnic site.

Quakers had a very liberal view of other people's religious beliefs and the Church of St John the Evangelist was built in 1863. Next to it was built the equally impressive and substantial school. There was also a Methodist chapel but obviously no pub was built directly within the confines of the village.

Continue along the substantial track to reach a T-junction.

④ Turn right onto a good farm track towards **Lower Landskill Farm** and then pass through a metal gate. A gentle rise leads to a cattle grid but there is also a gate as an alternative. This is the highest point on this walk and approaches another gate leading to Landskill Farm. Turn right at this point and cross the farmyard over some cobbles.

⑤ At this point the path divides. Be sure to take the right fork and go over another cattle grid which also has a gate close by – which is much appreciated by nervous dogs who are wary of negotiating the gaps in the cattle grid. Look for **Stirk Hey Cottage** and woodland.

'Stirk' means a young bull and 'Hey' indicates a woodland. This has long been summer grazing country and this is still the case. Here is another chance to enjoy the springtime bluebells but there are woodland delights at all times of the year with autumn colours and winter fungi also very much a feature.

The obvious track continues downhill to reach the Long Row and onto the starting point.

Around Fairhaven Lake, St Annes

Setting off.

A wonderful walk around an attractive lake and along the beach at St Annes. This will suit all sizes and fitness levels of dogs: old dogs can take their time to learn new tricks whilst boisterous hounds will not be short of areas to romp. This is a place to see the variety of bird life taking advantage of the sheltered area of the lake and its surroundings. For those taking puppies for their first walks, it is the perfect place to meet other dogs and allow them to mix and socialise.

Where to park

In the pay and display car park at Fairhaven Lake (GR SD344273). **OS Map:** OS Explorer 286 Blackpool & Preston.

How to get there

Leave the M55 motorway at Junction 4. Head to South Shore and follow the A5230. Continue until you see a large pale-coloured church on the right. Turn right following the Fairhaven Lake signs. Cross the A584 to the car park.

Refreshments

There is a snack bar, a café and plenty of seats along the route which are ideal for picnics.

The Walk

1 From the starting point, pass the snack bar, turn left and descend a solid set of stone steps to pass the toilets on the left.

2 Approach the **RSPB centre** which provides lots of useful information about the wildlife of the area. Visitors are made very welcome and entry is free. Also pass an attractive café which, in the early years of the last century, was the clubhouse of a golf club. Until a sea wall was built the course was often flooded and so it was replaced by a lake.

3 The route passes between the lake and a playground area including tennis, bowls, a children's area and a skateboard park. There are lots of seats and also red-coloured lifebelts at intervals.

4 At one of these lifebelts the track bears sharp left to follow a wide track leading back to the car park. Ignore this but look for a narrow path to the right which leads up to the beacon, high above the outer promenade, erected as a

Dog factors

Distance: 2½ miles.
Road walking: None.
Livestock: None.
Stiles: None.
Nearest vets: Veterinary Health Centre, Lytham St Annes.

Follow my leader!

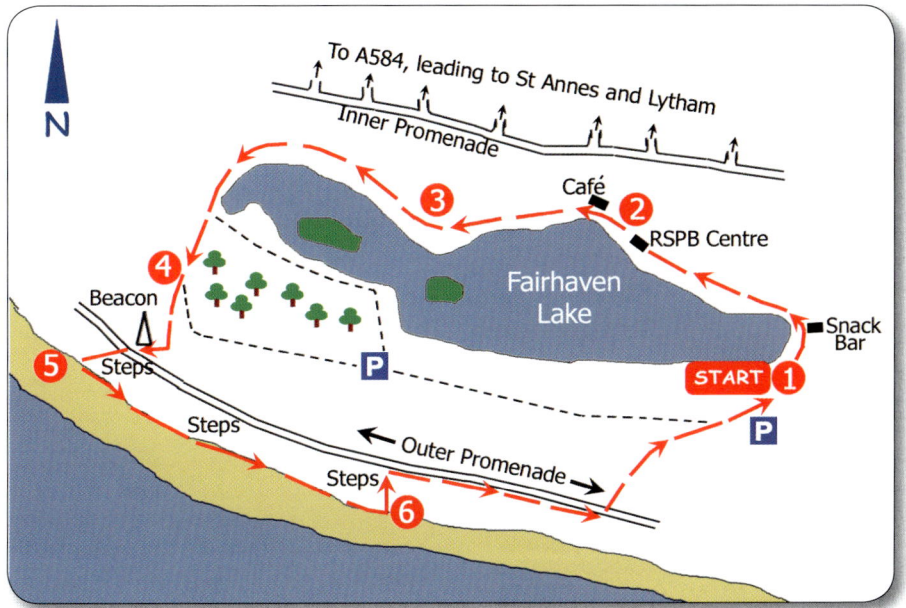

landmark to celebrate the Millennium. In this area there are secluded wooded areas for dogs to explore and also well-positioned picnic tables.

❺ At the beacon look out for some stone steps set into the sea wall. Descend these rough steps to reach the beach. To the right is a wide area of open sand, driftwood, seashells and seaweed. This is the place for owners to sit still and let the dogs run free. There is ample opportunity here to throw sticks and have them retrieved. After this interlude follow the sea wall along the beach.

Families with dogs can have a wonderful time. The shore is littered with a variety of seashells and the RSPB organise beach walks, which are especially popular with school parties on calm days following a storm when items of great interest have been washed ashore.

❻ Another set of stone steps let into the sea wall is reached. Ascend these steps to reach the outer promenade and return to the car park. Don't forget to have a towel and a drink of water ready for your dog.

Barley

![Black Moss reservoir]

Black Moss reservoir.

This is certainly the walk for dogs to make friends; and the stream and the picnic site are a delight for hounds of all shapes and sizes. The walk itself has reservoirs, woodlands and a pretty winding watercourse, with lots of deeper areas tailor-made for dogs.

Barley is an ancient settlement, known as Barelich as early as 1324. This literally means an infertile meadow and there were also a number of associated hamlets, two of which were called Wheatley Booth and Hay Booth with 'booth' meaning a cow farm. It tells us that cattle breeding was part of the economy and this is still the case today. In the 18th century Barley had a developing and thriving textile industry: first, handloom weaving was important and some of the cottages and farms clearly relate to this period.

From the village we walk up to the Black Moss reservoirs, built in the mid-19th century to provide water for the cotton mills of Nelson. This is kingfisher country and one of the best places to birdwatch in Lancashire whatever the season of the year, with pochard, tufted duck, great crested grebe and grey wagtail. Aitken Wood is being extensively replanted with native deciduous trees – this is Inka's favourite winter walk and chasing snowballs among the trees is her idea of canine heaven. The route returns through the lovely hamlet of Narrowgates.

Terrain

Uphill to the reservoirs and then largely downhill along a lane and few fields below Stang Moor Top.

Where to park

The pay and display car park near Barley Bridge (GR SD823403) where there is an information centre, toilets, café and an extensive picnic site. **OS map:** OL21 South Pennines

How to get there

Barley can be reached from the Nelson area (M65 Junction 13). Passing through Barrowford, turn left at the White Bear and ascend Pasture Lane. Dropping down into Roughlee, turn left at the Bay Horse and then right at a crossroads to Barley. The large car park is on the right. From Clitheroe along the A671 pass through Chatburn and follow signs to Downham. Follow the narrow road up and over Pendle Hill and down into Barley. Turn left at Barley Bridge and left into the pay and display car park.

Dog factors

· ·

Distance: 4 miles.
Road walking: 1 mile.
Livestock: Possibly cattle and sheep on field sections.
Stiles: None.
Nearest vets: Mearley Veterinary Group, Clitheroe.

Refreshments

In Barley there is the Barley Mow restaurant (☎ 01282 614293) and also a village café where dogs are welcome.

The Walk

· ·

1 Leave the car park and pass through the picnic area, and cross a footbridge into Barley village.

The fast flowing streams which run through the village were perfect for the development of water-powered cotton mills. Close to the Pendle Inn which was rebuilt in 1930 is a row of cottages which was constructed by dividing up the old hostelry itself. At the rear of the cottages the old inn yard can clearly be seen.

Continue along the narrow main street of the village and pass the Methodist chapel on the right.

2 Just beyond the chapel the road swings very sharply to the left but look out for a track leading off to the right. This leads to the **Black Moss reservoirs**. Apart from during the lambing season this is the time to let well-behaved dogs off the lead to absorb the smells of the countryside. The track ascends to the lower reservoir on the left: look out for the overflow weir which releases water to feed one of the streams that runs through Barley. Keep the reservoir, surrounded by stone walls to the left and bear right and uphill to approach the upper Black Moss reservoir.

3 Continue straight ahead along the reservoir track with the upper reservoir on the left. The track eventually leads to a lane at Black Moss Farm. Turn right along this lane and at the T-junction turn right and follow the adjoining Stang Top Road gradually uphill to the brow of the hill where there is a bridleway sign and gate on the right.

4 Go through the gate and join this bridleway which keeps below a trig point on the right and soon drops steeply downhill. The path turns sharp left and passes through more gates to join a lane by the Outdoor Education Centre at Whitehough. This has been operated by the local authority since 1938 – it may be as well to put your dog back on a lead here when children are about. Turn right downhill and pass through the hamlet to meet another access road..

5 Turn right and follow the access track with a pretty stream on your left. There are deeper pools ideal for paddling and much loved by children and dogs.

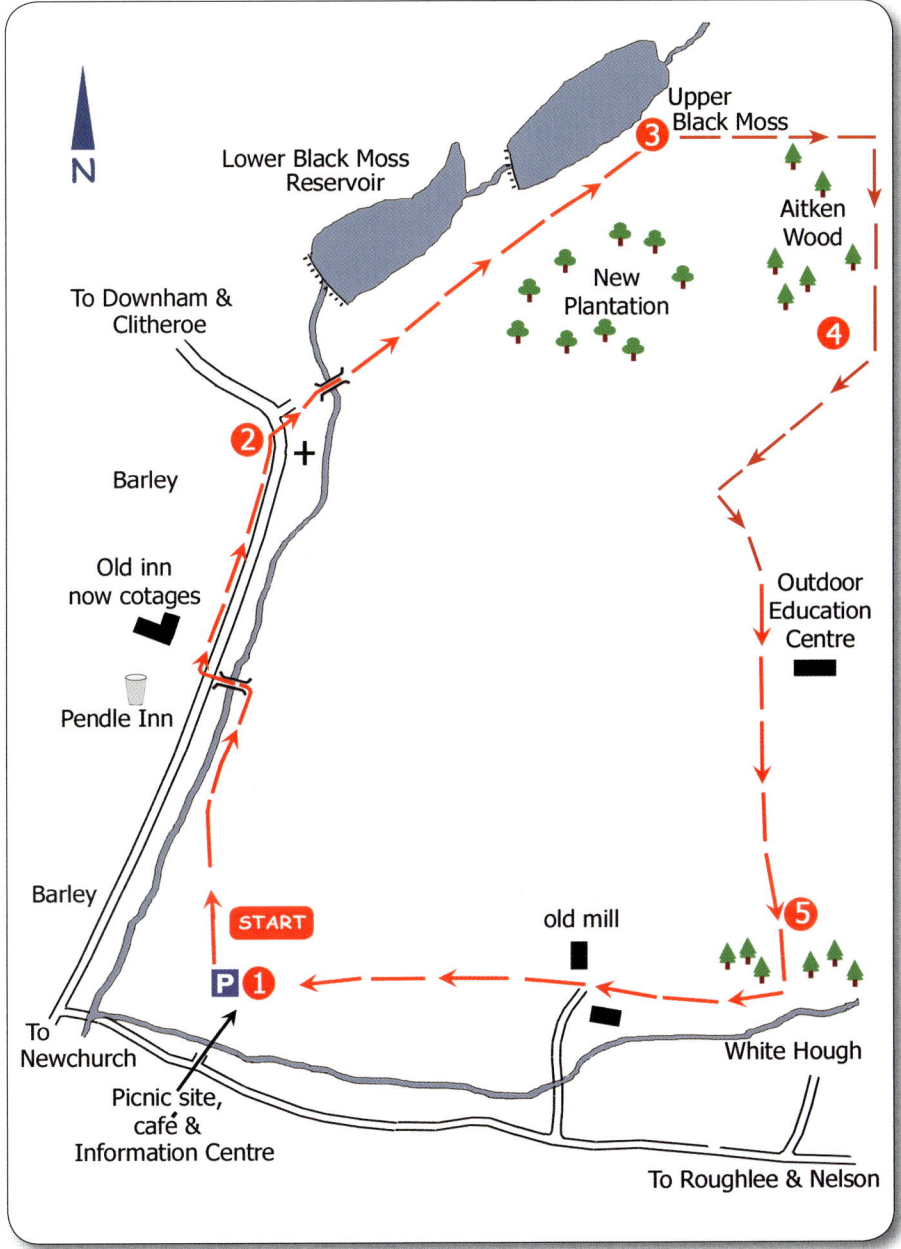

N

Lower Black Moss
Reservoir

Upper
Black Moss

③

Aitken
Wood

To Downham &
Clitheroe

④

New
Plantation

②

Barley

Old inn
now cotages

Pendle Inn

Outdoor
Education
Centre

Barley

START

old mill

⑤

P ①

To
Newchurch

Picnic site,
café &
Information Centre

White Hough

To Roughlee & Nelson

This is the breeding area for grey wagtails and dippers. Continue, to reach the now very pretty hamlet of **Narrowgates**.

In the 18th century William Hartley built what was known as a cotton twist mill here, which produced the thread used in the warp of a loom. Like all mill owners of the time, Hartley built cottages to attract workers and these have been restored and are privately owned. Part of the mill is now a private residence and the old chimney still dominates the settlement.

Pass through this little gem of a hamlet and continue back to the starting point at the car park.

Aitken Wood seen from the route.

Ribchester, Stydd and Kellets

Approaching Stydd Manor farm complex.

There are literally 'legions' of fascinating aspects to this stroll, which follows in the footsteps of the Roman army as they had a substantial fort on the banks of the Ribble. The route leads up, over and around medieval dewponds, Norman churches, Roman roads and tracks even more ancient and probably dating back to the Bronze Age. There are also panoramic views from Duddel Hill to enjoy, and the lovely countryside around Knowle Green.

In 2010 the Environment Agency launched a plan to restore as many old ponds as possible. These dewponds were once vital to the survival of farm animals before the days of piped water and all farmers kept them in good order. What a boon it would be if these old reminders of our countryside could be restored. Here there are several dewponds and this walk is a good route to take after rain. With Inka being so fond of mud, she is well able to enjoy these ponds. At the end of the walk she needs a large container full of water, a towel and an old blanket in the back of the car! It also makes sense to add a few biscuits.

Terrain

Mostly easy walking, with a steep climb towards the summit of Duddel Hill. Depending on the weather, there may be ponds and small streams along the way.

Where to park

Ribchester village centre pay and display car park (GR SD649352). **OS map:** Explorer 287 West Pennine Moors.

How to get there

Take the A59 linking Preston with Clitheroe. At the traffic lights between Osbaldeston and Copster Green turn left and descend towards Ribchester. Pass over a substantial bridge across the River Ribble. Follow the road through the village and take the signs for the car park.

Refreshments

There are plenty of hostelries and cafés in the village and there is also a picnic site opposite the car park.

The Walk

. . . .

1 From the car park turn left. On the left is a tearoom and on the right a children's playground and picnic site.

Dog factors

. . . .

Distance: 4½ miles.
Road walking: About ½ mile.
Livestock: Occasional.
Stiles: 10, two with which less agile dogs may need some assistance .
Nearest vets: 'My Vet', Clayton-le-Dale.

These areas were once the parade ground where the Roman soldiers trained and drilled. Here is a memorial garden built to celebrate the Millennium and where there is a display of sculptures telling the history of the Roman fort which had no fewer than 500 cavalrymen in residence during the first century AD.

Turn right into Church Street and look for the **White Bull Hotel** on the left. The porch is supported by a set of Roman pillars which may well have graced a temple. Turn left along **Water Street** and divert slightly to the right.

2 Explore the **Roman bathhouse** situated close to the river and around which dogs can wander but should be kept on a lead. Continue along **Water Street** to reach the **Ribchester Arms**. Turn right and continue through the village to reach **Stydd Lane**.

3 Continue along **Stydd Lane** to reach a splendid set of almshouses.

These were built in 1728 by the Shireburn family of Stonyhurst, their former mansion now being the base for a Roman Catholic public school. Look carefully at the almshouses and marvel at a set of steps supported by a balustrade and pillars which look like a 'blast from the past' of ancient Rome.

4 Ascend a well-made track to reach a chapel on the right.

This dates to the 12th century and has a fine Norman doorway. It was built by the Knights Hospitallers, an organisation dating back to the Crusades when their members protected pilgrims during their journey to and from Palestine. The Knights were part soldiers and part medical men and it is to them that we owe the words hospitality and hospital. They were skilled herbalists and it is well worth exploring the area around the chapel which was once their herb garden. Plants such as betony, self heal and St John's wort all had their uses all those years ago.

5 At the **Stydd Manor** farm complex pass close to the farmyard and go through two gates to reach a field. The route here climbs steeply and there is a hedge full of 'doggie smells' on the right. When you reach a gate and a stile, ignore the gate and climb the stile. There is now a hedge on the left. Cross a small footbridge and continue to climb through a lush field, and here there is another stile to be negotiated. Look to the left to see an ancient dewpond which has now sadly dried up.

*The highest point of this walk is the 410 ft (125m) summit of **Duddel Hill** and human beings may like to pause here and look at the panoramic view of Longridge Fell immediately in front and Pendle Hill to the right.*

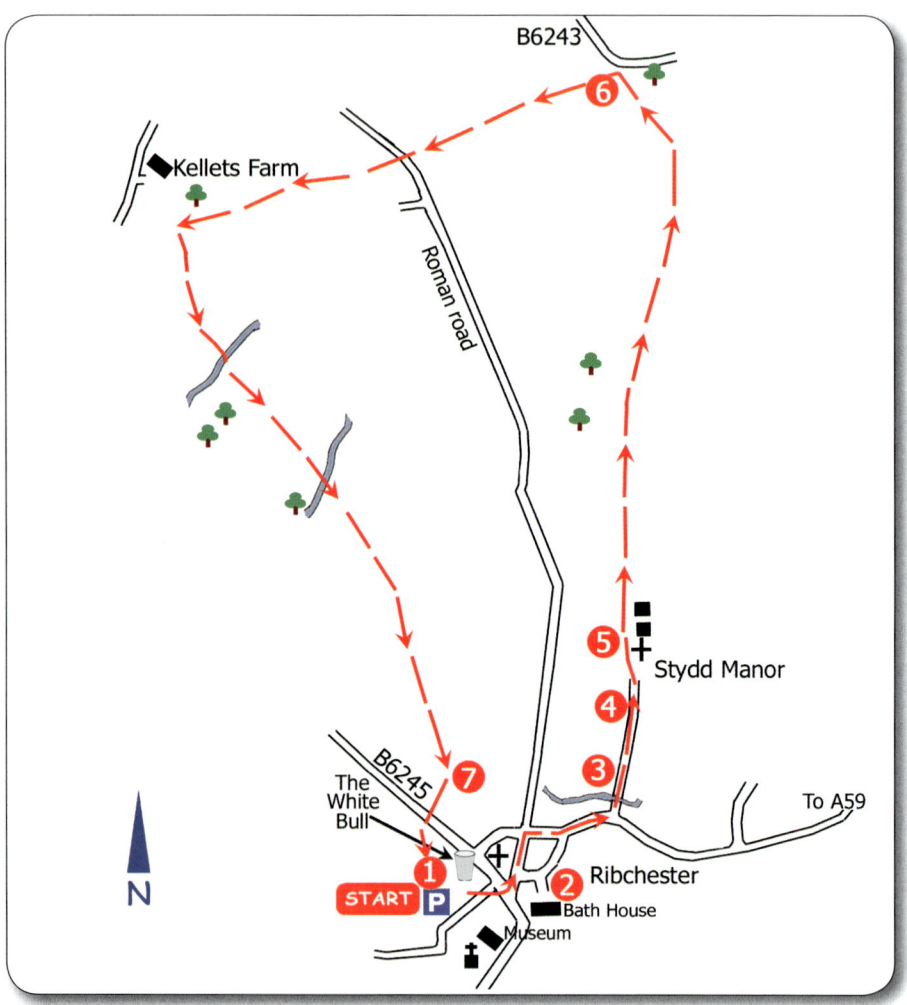

6 Descend a sunken track towards a farmhouse. Pass through a gate and follow the drive, which is on the direct line of the old Roman road, to the B6243.

The area around Kellets is a joyful mixture of fields and trees, and the nearby hamlet of Knowle Green is also a fascinating place. Knowle Green itself is now just a hamlet but it was once directly on the Roman road linking Ribchester and Overbarrow on the River Lune. In Knowle Green is the strange Written Stone which reads 'Ravffe Radcliffe laid this stone to Lye forever 1655'. Apart from the fact that it is 11 feet long and 18 inches wide, nothing is known about it and it is one of Lancashire's unexplained mysteries.

Cross the B6243 but do not join this road, instead soon turn left.

This is best described as 'stile country' but they present few problems. Depending upon the rainfall there are small streams here, one of which is best negotiated by a little footbridge unless you are a dog, in which case here is a chance to get rid of any excess mud!

Descend through stiles and past tiny streams lined by trees, with dewponds appearing especially during wet weather.

7 The track bears right to reach the B6245. Turn left to return to the village car park.

The 12th-century Stydd chapel.

Towneley

'What's that in the bushes?'

This is a very enjoyable 'half and half' walk. Most of Burnley's parks are sadly no-go areas for dogs but Towneley is a most welcome and very popular exception. At the start of the walk is a huge area of playing fields where dogs can roam free and then comes the Thanet Lee woodland which is full of smells and sounds to provide canine fun. The scenery is wonderful with sweeping views of the ever-cleaner River Calder away to the right. The route then climbs to Foldys Cross, a 15th-century market cross brought here to the park and overlooking Towneley Hall.

There are streams in the woodland area, ideal for a doggie paddle, which are irresistible to Labradors and some other breeds. The second part of the walk requires dogs to be on leads but they will already have let off steam. If the lead is long enough, there are plenty of smells for pooches to enjoy. Whatever the weather or whatever the season, this walk offers variety, beauty and areas of splendid seclusion.

Terrain

Generally easy and flat but there is one steep incline leading up to point 5 of the walk.

Where to park

The short stay car park (small fee by the hour) opposite Towneley Hall (GR SD856307). **OS map:** OL21 South Pennines.

How to get there

Towneley Park is situated close to the town centre of Burnley and reached along the A671 road (Todmorden Road) close to Turf Moor Football Stadium. Travelling south approach a set of traffic lights and a mini-roundabout and follow a sign to the left leading to the grounds. Pass a school on the right and a new college on the left. Bear right with a golf course on the right.

Refreshments

The Old Stables Café at Towneley Hall (☎ 01282 424213) serves hot and cold meals of a high standard and a modest price. There are outside benches where dogs are allowed. There are also seats on the route where picnics can be enjoyed.

Dog factors

Distance: 2½ miles.
Road walking: None.
Livestock: There are areas in Thanet Lee and on the playing fields where horses add to the variety of the area and the equestrians are mostly used to dogs being around but dog owners do need to understand the temperament of their pets.
Stiles: None.
Nearest vets: Oakmount Veterinary Centre, Burnley.

The Walk

1. From the car park, turn away from the hall and follow a track. The first turning on the left leads into **Thanet Lee Wood** which has a circular trail running around it. Roe deer are becoming increasingly common whilst the bird life is always rich, including the greater spotted woodpecker, jay, tawny owl, sparrowhawk and an occasional woodcock.

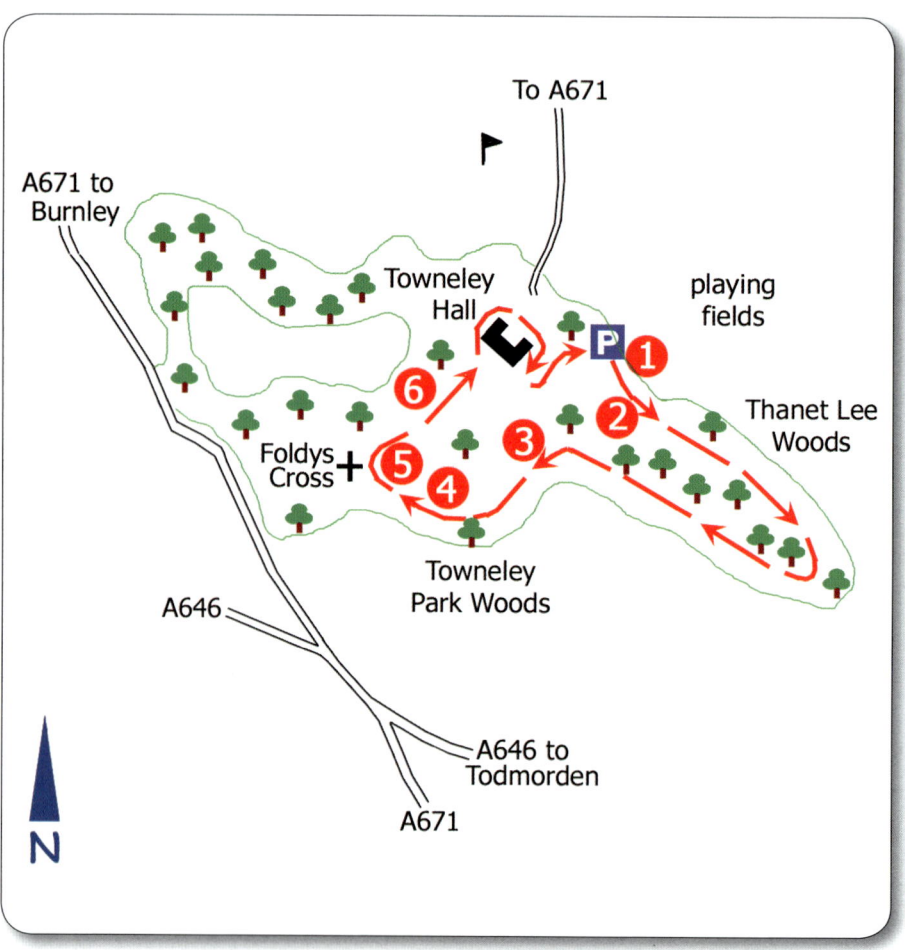

2 Enter the wood, which is a doggie delight. Cross a bridge over a tributary stream of the **River Calder**.

Here is an expanse of pool and mud. Over the last 30 years I have had three Labradors, with Inka the latest in the line: black Labrador and brown mud produces a combination which only those who love dogs can understand!

Follow the circular path around the extensive deciduous woodland to reach a small bridge over a stream. This meets a track; turn right and after a short distance left into **Towneley Park woods**.

Towneley Hall seen from the lake.

3 After about 100 yards pass under a little bridge and at this point dogs should be put on extender leads. This is deciduous woodland at its very best and enough lead should be allowed to give your pets 'sniffing space'.

Look out to the left to see a sign indicating Burnley's oldest tree, an oak set in splendid isolation in a field seen through a gap in a fence. The sign points out that this is at least 400 years old and it still looks in prime condition.

4 Continue along a steepish incline passing a bird reserve surrounded by a protective fence, which was established in the 1970s.

Here is the place to listen as well as look for breeding jay, greater spotted woodpecker and occasionally sparrowhawks. Tawny owls are also resident. This area and Thanet Lee have long been a mecca for local birdwatchers.

5 At the crest of the ridge is the impressive **Foldys Cross**. From the steps look straight ahead and down to **Towneley Hall**.

John Foldys was the chaplain to the vicar of Burnley in the 15th century and he was responsible for the erection of a market cross close to St Peter's church. The cross is impressive and is surmounted by a set of steps. Inka looks forward to visiting these steps because she loves waiting to see the grey squirrels which seem to find them equally fascinating.

Parts of Towneley Hall date to the 14th century but most is Elizabethan. It was a family home until Lady O'Hagan (neé Towneley) sold the hall and grounds comprising 360 acres to Burnley Town Council at a modest fee in 1902. Since then it has been the town's museum and art gallery. In 2009–10 a millennium grant was sensibly spent and the grounds and gardens are now looking at their best.

6 Descend to the hall and keep the building on the right. Pass a toilet block and craft museum converted from the old brew house. Sweep right to the front of the hall and see the **Old Stables Café** and pond on the left. At the end of the hall turn sharp right to find the colourful gardens on the left. Here are lots of seats ideal for a quiet sit, providing your canine companion will let you.

7 Turn left and look out for a large stone on the right.

This is called an erratic and was carried here from the Lake District by glaciers as the last Ice Age loosened its grip during a much earlier period of global warming. There is an inscription on the stone dedicated to the memory of Clifford Oakes (1895–1946), a famous ornithologist who wrote The Birds of Lancashire.

Return from the stone and head back past the war memorial to reach the car park. If your dog is not quite worn out, another chase around the playing fields should do the trick and ensure a quiet night at home!

Clowbridge and Gambleside

Clowbridge reservoir is home to Rossendale Valley Sailing Club.

It is hard to believe that the area now occupied by the reservoir was once a thriving community called Gambleside. This walk is a fascinating stroll by the reservoir to the former coal mining area and the atmospheric ruins of the village. Time should be taken here and this walk is particularly interesting in winter when the vegetation has died down and the remnants of the old settlement can more clearly be seen.

There are records of a settlement at Gambleside at least from 1507 when its income was derived from farming, limestone quarrying, coal mining and handloom weaving. Look out for a depression marking the old road linking the Ribble Valley with Rochdale. This was accurately called the 'holloway' and for those who do not rush this walk, stretches can still be seen. Holloways were created as the horse traffic along them wore the surfaces down over the course of centuries.

Initially this walk looks to be anything but dog-friendly because the marked circular trail around the Clowbridge reservoir is forbidden to dogs by United Utilities, the water company. However, they have compensated for this by developing access around the area and all my dogs have enjoyed following this walk.

Terrain

A short and simple walk, over moorland and through woodland.

Where to park

The large pay and display car park near Rossendale Valley Sailing Club (GR SD823280). **OS map:** OL21 South Pennines.

How to get there

Clowbridge reservoir is situated close to the A682 which connects Burnley to Rawtenstall. At Dunnockshaw hamlet a not very obvious sign on the left leads onto the substantial track on the left to the Rossendale Valley Sailing Club and the suggested car park for the walk.

Refreshments

None on the route, so take a picnic or visit one of the many hostelries to be found in Burnley, Rawtenstall or along the road between the two.

The Walk

. . . .

1 From the far extremity of the car park, look out for a short flight of stone steps. Ascend these and follow the gentle incline up a twisting track to the right and approach the **Rossendale Valley Sailing Club**.

Dog factors

. . . .

Distance: 2 miles.
Road walking: None.
Livestock: None.
Stiles: None, but one gate.
Nearest vets: Oakmount Veterinary Centre, Burnley.

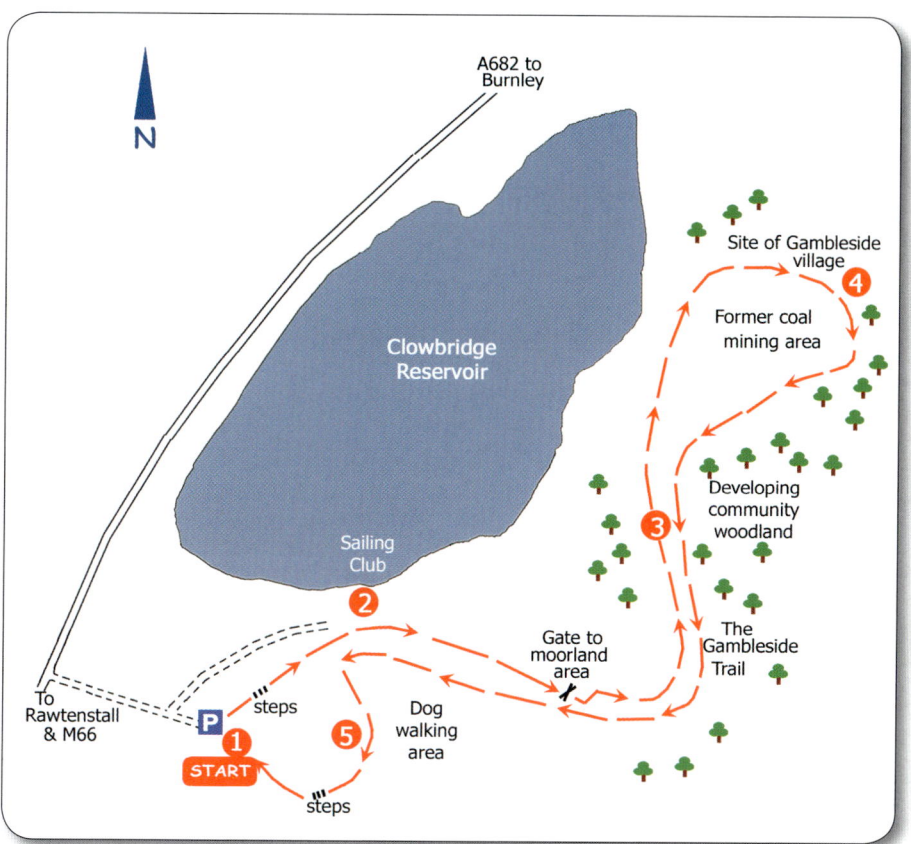

2 There is a footpath to the left which circles the reservoir but this is a dog no-go area. Dogs are, however, welcome on the track to the right. Follow the gentle incline to reach a gate. Stop to look at the display board depicting the history of Gambleside from both domestic and industrial aspects. This damp moorland area is meant for dogs to enjoy and 'poo boxes' are provided.

3 The track bears left and approaches the reservoir to the left.

This is the former coal mining area. Mining went on for much longer than the hamlet. The main shaft had a pumping pit, which kept the workings free from flooding. This was situated close to the modern day reservoir's pump house. In the 19th century the pit had a boiler and engine house, workshop, offices and a very primitive changing room. The coal seams were so difficult to work that boys as young as six and called drawers moved into very confined spaces to fill the tubs with coal. All miners were paid on piece rates and Gambleside did not cease its operations until 1936.

4 The route now offers the chance for you and your dog to explore the developing community woodland.

The Community Woodland project has been part of the Forest of Burnley planting scheme and around Gambleside upwards of 2,000 native trees have been planted.
*Away to the right is **Clowbridge reservoir** which provides an excellent winter birdwatch, with species such as wigeon, goosander, goldeneye, tufted duck and great crested grebe usually present.*

Follow the return track to reach the gate and the Gambleside display board where there is also is a board explaining the work of the Community Woodland project.

5 Descend to the left and look out from the track to the left. Here is a sign indicating the dog walking area, a real bonus for dogs. The route twists and turns as it descends through mature trees and returns to the car park.

Walkers returning from the circular trail.

Around Roach Bridge

The weir at Roach Bridge.

This walk follows field and woodland paths around the hamlet of Coup Green, crossing the Beeston Brook and the River Darwen. This is now heron, kingfisher, dipper and grey wagtail territory with all four species resident in the area. In the summer oystercatchers and common sandpipers breed by the riverside and in winter there are often wildfowl to see. The deep stretches of river are very attractive to goosander, goldeneye and the occasional long-tailed duck.

Roach Bridge Paper Mill, where the walk begins, was built in the 19th century. Paper making requires a reliable source of fresh water. Despite pollution the paper mill survived until recent times and although it is now ruined the building has maintained its impressive architecture and is very much part of the industrial archaeology of the area. In recent years pollution levels have been considerably reduced and it is now safe for dogs to splash in the watercourses, and fish including trout have returned to their former haunts.

Lancashire – A Dog Walker's Guide

Terrain

Although there is some road walking, this is along fairly quiet areas. There are some boggy areas close to the River Darwen and especially around one of its tributaries which is Beeston Brook but these are easily negotiated. A steady but quite steep ascent after point 2.

Where to park

On the road near the New Hall Tavern in Roach Bridge (GR SD594292). **OS map:** Explorer 286 Blackpool & Preston.

How to get there

From the A59 at Samlesbury, follow the signs to Roach Bridge. An alternative route is to follow the B6230 which links Walton-le-Dale and Samlesbury. The New Hall Tavern will be found at a crossroads..

Refreshments

The New Hall Tavern (☎ 01772 877942) has just had a facelift and has resisted the modern trend where so many hostelries have been forced to close. There are also plenty of farm shops, pubs and restaurants on the A59.

The Walk

• •

1 From the crossroads at the old New Hall Tavern head downhill to reach the ruins of the paper mill at **Roach Bridge**. Cross the **River Darwen** at this point. There is now a slight incline at the end of the mill complex. Look out for a bridleway signed to the left. This is not used very often by equestrians but dog owners do need to keep a wary eye and ear open for horses. There is now a steady but quite steep ascent through a substantial belt of trees. Here there is always a plentiful supply of sticks. Enter a field and keep the trees to your right. A track leads towards a group of farm buildings. Do not go through the farmyard but keep a look out for a stile in the corner of the field.

Dog factors

• •

Distance: 3½ miles.
Road walking: ¾ mile along quiet roads.
Livestock: Minimal, but some grazing cattle in the summer and possibly horses on the bridleway.
Stiles: 7, but all negotiable.
Nearest vets: Abbeyvale Veterinary Centre, Blackburn.

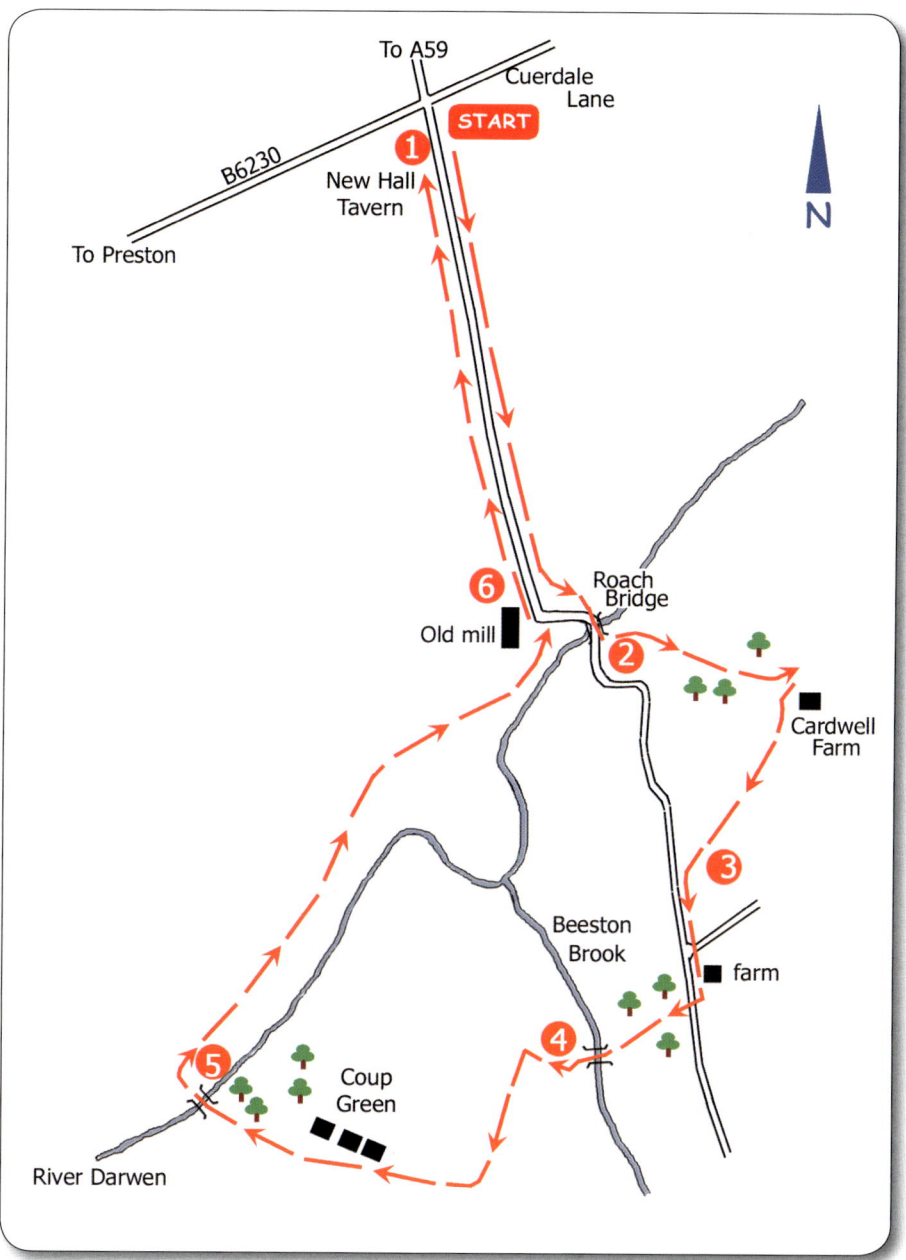

To A59

Cuerdale Lane

START

B6230

To Preston

1 New Hall Tavern

N

6 Old mill

Roach Bridge

2

Cardwell Farm

3

Beeston Brook

farm

4

5

Coup Green

River Darwen

Lancashire – A Dog Walker's Guide

2 Cross the stile and bear very slightly to the left above a wooded incline. Pass through fields and follow the well-marked signs. Turn left at a gate leading to a substantial track and descend still following the marked indicators. This leads into a very pretty lane.

3 Turn sharp left at this point and ascend for about 400 yards. Do not follow the road junction to the left but continue onwards to reach a cottage and a small farm. Immediately opposite is a substantial and easily negotiated stile. Cross this to join a field which leads to another stile. Follow ahead to reach another wooded area. Approach a footbridge over **Beeston Brook**.

4 Cross the footbridge and firstly bear right to approach a steep bank leading to another lush and often damp field. The route heads for a group of houses making up the hamlet of **Coup Green**. Dogs do need to be on a lead for a short distance here in order to negotiate the pavements in the hamlet. This soon evolves into a track, which descends into steep woodland which means that dogs are now happier. Pass a farm on the left and the route continues to descend to reach a substantial stone bridge over the **River Darwen**.

5 Cross this bridge and follow the obvious riverside track to the right. Cross a stone stile and follow a well-marked public footpath leading into yet another lush damp field. This is paddle country for dogs. The riverside path leads to a cascade where the Darwen flows quickly over a number of red coloured rocks. Follow onwards to reach a stile as the river meanders to the right. Cross another stile and then the river diverts to the left to approach close to the footpath again. In the summer cattle may graze in this area and dog owners need to be aware of this but in the winter months this is not a problem. Cross another stile to reach **Roach Bridge**.

6 At **Roach Bridge** turn left and return uphill to the starting point. Time, however, should be taken at the bridge to enjoy the wildlife in and around the river.

New Hall Tavern, at the start of the walk.

I well remember the second of my labradors (Bono) would not leave the bridge to return to the starting point until he had returned to the trees. There he would select a huge stick and once at home in front of the fire he reduced his log into splinters which eventually fuelled flames.

Hoghton

The approach to Hoghton Tower.

Stretches of open countryside, woodland, riverside, and a magnificent wooded gorge, all set around one of the earliest estate villages in England, give this walk something for everybody.

Hoghton literally means 'a township at the bottom of a hill'. The de Hoghtons came from Normandy with William the Conqueror's army in 1066. The baronetcy is the second oldest in the country and the site has been in the same family ever since. Hoghton Tower still stands, a fortified hilltop mansion 560 ft (170 m) above sea level. It is open to the public during the warmer months and specific events are often organised. William Shakespeare is believed to have worked here as a young actor. Another claim to fame was in 1617 when James I visited Hoghton and was entertained to a massive feast. He was apparently so pleased with the beef that he raised his sword to the joint and proclaimed it 'Sir Loin'. The table where this ceremony took place is on display in the Tower. There is still a local tradition of serving good meat and there is even a hostelry called the Sirloin.

Lancashire – A Dog Walker's Guide

Terrain

From Hoghton the route ascends the track to the Tower, then returns downhill to Hoghton Bottoms and the River Darwen. Take care when crossing the railway line in point 2.

Where to park

On-street near the Boars Head (GR SD613267). **OS map:** Explorer 287 West Pennine Moors.

How to get there

The village is situated directly on the A675 between Blackburn and Preston.

Refreshments

Pubs in the village include the Boars Head (☎ 01254 852272) and the Sirloin (☎ 01254 852293). There are also places locally selling pies and sandwiches and there are plenty of places to picnic. The route passes the Royal Oak at Riley Green (☎ 01254 201445), an impressive example of an old coaching inn offering a warm welcome to visitors.

Dog factors

Distance: 3 miles.
Road walking: Minimal.
Livestock: Very occasional cattle and sheep.
Stiles: 7, one a substantial ladder stile where less agile dogs may need a little help.
Nearest vets: Hillcrest Animal Hospital, Chorley.

The Walk

1 From the **Boars Head** turn left along the A675 to reach the war memorial and close to this is the wide driveway leading up to **Hoghton Tower**. Turn left and ascend the track towards the tower. At the lodge gates bear left.

2 Follow an obvious track to reach a stile. Cross this and keep a wall to the right and with fields in front. Cross two more stiles and then head downhill to a belt of trees to reach the still operative **railway** which links Preston and Blackburn. This was built in the 1840s. Cross this with care and it goes without saying that dogs need to be on a close lead.

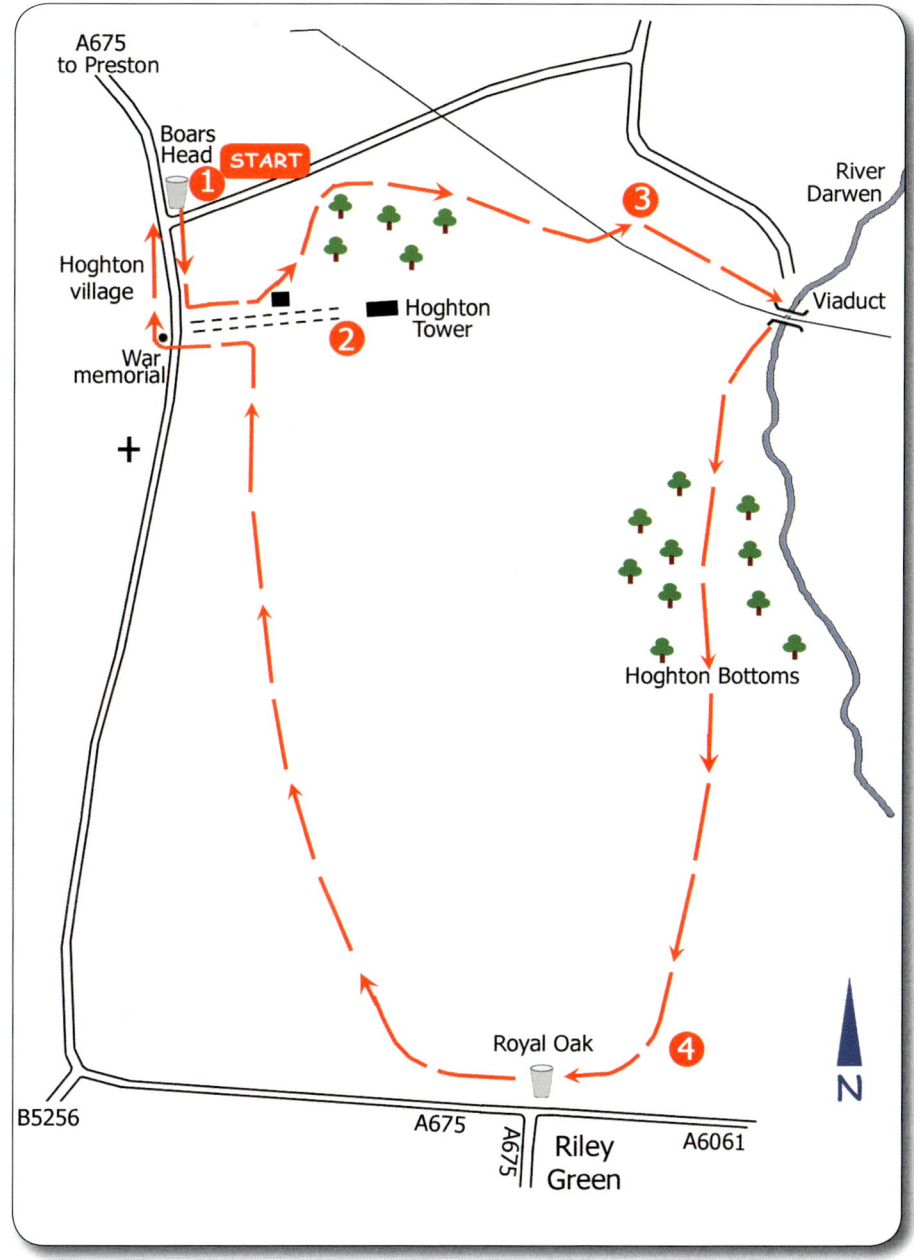

3 Turn right and ignore a more obvious bend to the left. Continue straight ahead close to the river to reach a substantial and magnificent wooded gorge. Pass underneath an amply-proportioned, five-arched viaduct crossing over the **River Darwen** some 116 ft (35 m) below. You are now at **Hoghton Bottoms** and the Gregson Lane area, where there are some 'splashing areas' for dogs.

'Are you ready yet?'

This area has long been steeped in Roman Catholicism and it is said that William Shakespeare spent a year at Hoghton Tower because of his faith. Whether this was the reason for his sojourn is not proved but it does seem certain that he was employed as a young actor under the name of William Shakeshaft. It was also here that the priest Edmund Arrowsmith said his last mass, in a house now bearing an inscription to this effect, before he was arrested and executed on the orders of Elizabeth I. A sideboard used in this mass now forms the altar of St Joseph's Roman Catholic church in the hamlet. Another religious building of note close to the railway bridge on Chapel Lane is a Methodist chapel dated to 1794, one of the earliest dedicated to this sect to be set up in England.

Look out for a substantial ladder stile. The track then veers to the right away from the river. There is another obvious track here which leads to a kissing gate. Go through this and approach the A6061 road with care.

4 Turn right into yet another historic settlement at **Riley Green**. This substantial hamlet had the advantage of being firstly on the old turnpike road linking Blackburn and Preston and then on the line of the Leeds and Liverpool Canal, which was cut from Blackburn and Chorley. Just past the **Royal Oak** turn right along a good track leading to another substantial ladder stile and ascend gently with good views up to Hoghton Tower slightly to the right. At the summit of this track negotiate another stile and continue through lush countryside to reach another stile. Neither of these two are difficult obstacles for dogs. After yet another substantial stile the route now begins to descend to reach a kissing gate which leads to the driveway to **Hoghton Tower**. Turn right and return to the starting point.

Anglezarke and Clough

'Is it this way?'

This is a walk through history involving lead mining, early industrial chemistry and memories of the Second World War. It is also a delightful route for dogs.

The area around Anglezarke is full of 19th-century reservoirs built to supply water to the cotton towns in the Bolton area. The name, however, dates back to pre-Norman Old English when a chieftain called Anlaf had his power base here. From Anglezark we head for the Woodland Trail – at one time the quarries were used as spectacular sets for the television series *The Jewel in the Crown*, but the Woodland Trail is a modern-day jewel. Going out onto open moorland, you can make a short detour to the memorial raised to a Wellington bomber lost on the moor in 1943. I have heard that some dog owners would not visit Lead Mines Clough because of the fear of pollution. This is not the case these days and the stream is completely clean. Dogs love it and they can splash about and get rid of the mud collected on the wet moorland.

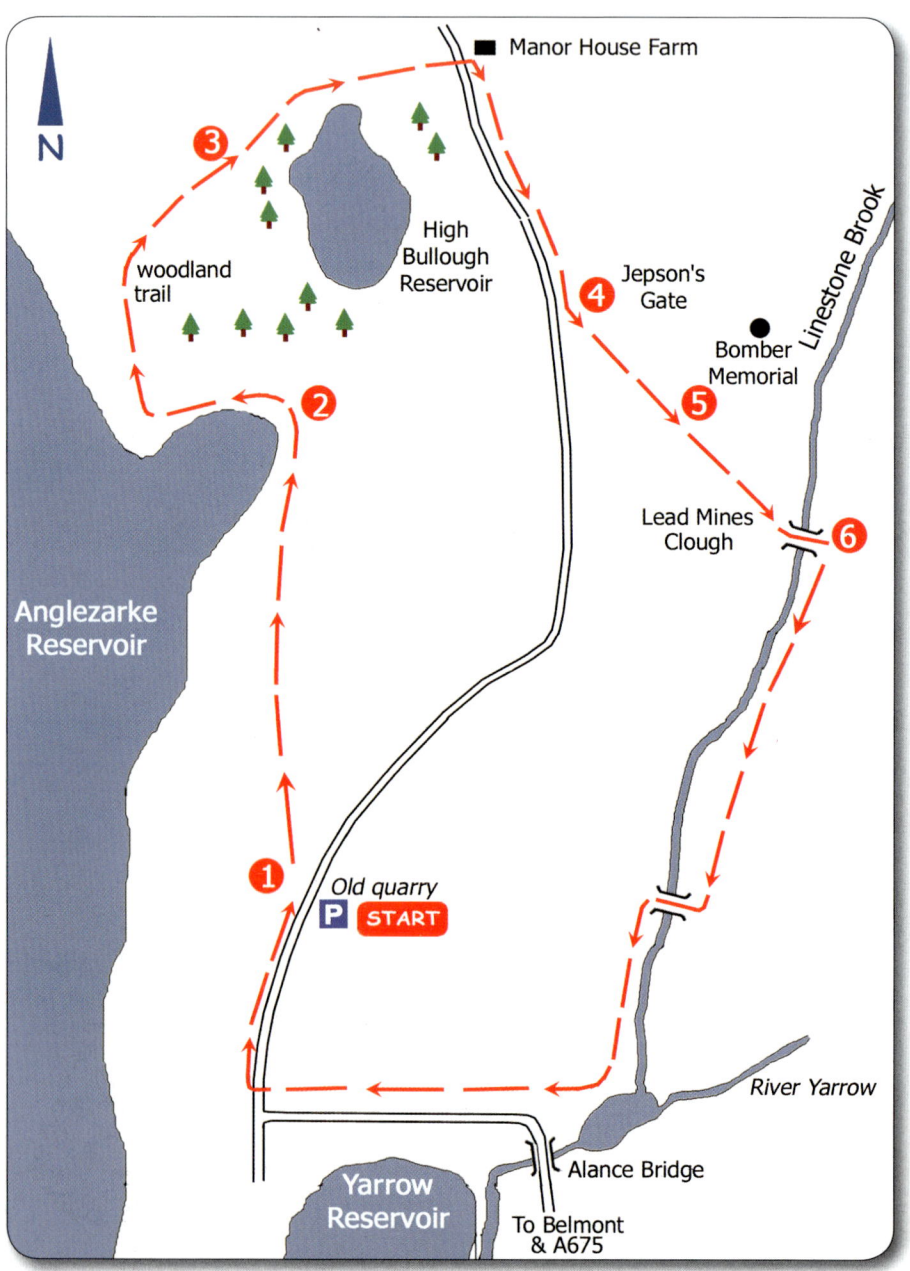

N

Manor House Farm

Linestone Brook

③

woodland
trail

High
Bullough
Reservoir

Jepson's
Gate

④

Bomber
Memorial

⑤

②

Lead Mines
Clough

⑥

Anglezarke
Reservoir

①

Old quarry

P START

River Yarrow

Alance Bridge

Yarrow
Reservoir

To Belmont
& A675

Terrain

Keep dogs on a lead close to the quarries and climbing areas which are well signed. There are a couple of steep tracks to take slowly.

Where to park

The pay and display car park at Anglezarke (GR SD620160). **OS map:** Explorer 287 West Pennine Moors.

How to get there

From the A675 Bolton to Blackburn road, turn left at Belmont and follow the minor road to reach Rivington village. Then bear right and follow the very narrow road to Anglezarke.

Refreshments

There are cafés in Rivington but many dog walkers prefer to take a picnic, with doggie bits added to the menu.

The Walk

. . . .

1 From the car park do not follow the Anglezarke Trail sign but pass through a gap and follow an obvious tarmac path. Look for a sign labelled **'Woodland Trail'** and descend this to reach a junction of paths. Turn right and pass through a quarry area which leads close to the banks of **Anglezarke reservoir**. Turn right for a short distance and follow the Woodland Trail.

2 Turn left to reach an information board and a seat, which is an ideal location to enjoy a picnic and think about the history of the quarries and the use which has been made of them in recent times.

Dog factors

. . . .

Distance: 3½ miles.
Road walking: Minimal.
Livestock: None but there is a short bridlepath so there is a need to keep an eye open for horses. The only area where strict supervision is needed is at the start of the walk where old quarries are now used by climbers and it would obviously be dangerous to spoil their concentration.
Stiles: 2, but easily negotiated.
Nearest vets: Pike Moor Vets, Horwich.

Lancashire – A Dog Walker's Guide

The Lister Mill quarries in particular have been used as a training ground for serious climbers, including Sir Chris Bonnington. Why Lister Mill? This dates back to the 18th century when Roger Lister set up an early textile mill powered by a local stream which now feeds the reservoir system. The quarries did a roaring trade in the 19th century when thousands of paving stones were produced to build the streets of industrial towns of northern Britain.

Follow an elevated path around the headland of the reservoir and continue for around ½ mile. The route then descends to merge with a second footpath and this is a perfect habitat for energetic dogs. Cross over this path leading towards Manor House Farm which can be seen high up on the moorland area.

3 Continue ahead and alongside a stone wall. Approach the **High Bullough Reservoir** which is one of the smallest in the area but is still an attractive place to birdwatch. The hillside here is quite steep but take your time to reach a footpath signed 'Manor House Farm'. Cross a field to reach a minor road and follow it for around 400 yards to reach a sharp bend. Follow the signs to **Jepson's Gate**, which leads to a wide bridleway onto the open moor. Dog owners should be aware that this is a bridleway and so need to keep an eye open for horses. Follow the signs to Jepson's Gate and head onto the moor.

4 Follow this route to reach the third of the gates and descend to the right through a damp – and sometimes wet – area of meadowland. I always label this as a dog mud bath! Divert slightly to the left to view the **Wellington Bomber memorial**. The tragedy occurred in 1943 on Hurst Hill.

5 A steep, winding and very narrow track leads from the memorial down into **Lead Mines Clough** which is sited alongside the well-named **Limestone Brook.**

Most historians believe that the Romans mined lead here in the 2nd century AD and the final shaft was only sealed in the 1930s. It seems likely that some clandestine activity took place here in the Second World War when preparations were being made to repel a possible German invasion force, with specially trained local men with a knowledge of explosives and the terrain detailed to hide in the old workings and fight in the hills.

Apart from lead mining a mineral called Witherite was discovered in the area in the 1780s. Most of it was purchased by the potter Josiah Wedgwood who used it amid great secrecy to perfect the colouring which we now know as Jasperware.

6 Cross a bridge and follow an obvious track downstream. Go over a second footbridge to join a minor track at **Alance Bridge**. Continue to ascend the minor road, keeping the reservoir on the left, to return to the starting point.

White Coppice

Fishing on the Old Mill Pond.

Looking at **White Coppice today** you could be forgiven for thinking it looks like a Tudor village, undisturbed apart from the construction of a cricket ground with its impressive pavilion. Yet White Coppice did flirt with industry and had a cotton mill in the very early days of the Industrial Revolution. It also had its tranquillity disturbed during the 19th century when reservoirs were built to slake the thirst of the ever-greedy King Cotton. One of these old mill ponds is now very popular with fishermen and their ever-patient canine friends. Before the mill lodge was built to provide water for the steam engine the machinery was powered by a waterwheel turned by the stream. Around 1900 the mill was owned by Alfred Ephraim Eccles who seems to have been something of a martinet. He operated from his house at Northwood and was a fearless – or should I say fearsome – supporter of the Temperance movement. It would not bode well for any of his workers who enjoyed a tipple!

Dog factors

Distance: 3 miles.
Road walking: Minimal.
Livestock: Little, if any.
Stiles: 4, easily negotiated.
Nearest vets: Hillcrest Animal Hospital, Chorley.

This circular stroll starts from the cricket ground, follows the line of the Goit, a beautiful artificial waterway, towards Anglezarke reservoir, undulates to reach the great viewpoint at Healey Nab and returns to the starting point through more lush woodland. For dogs this is a real treat because there are open spaces to run about in and sticks to chase, and owners can relax because their pets can be seen easily along the route.

Terrain

Very few stretches of road, which are quiet and more like tracks. There is a steep climb to Healey Nab but the views are a great excuse to stop and catch your breath.

Where to park

Between the nursery and the cricket field in White Coppice (GR SD620191). **OS map:** Explorer 287 West Pennine Moors.

How to get there

From Blackburn follow the A674 towards Chorley. Pass through Withnell Fold and look for a left turn to White Coppice. Find the old Railway pub (now a private dwelling) and then turn right into the cul-de-sac village of White Coppice. From the M61, exit at the Chorley turn and follow the A674 signed Blackburn. White Coppice is signed off the road to the right.

Refreshments

There are pubs along the A674 but why not take a picnic, plus a drink for the hound?

The Walk

1 Begin with a leisurely exploration of the hamlet with the dog on the lead (poo bags are essential because this is a lovely tidy village with old cottages set around an unpolluted little stream). Look out for the old mill lodge which is now a popular haunt of birdwatchers and anglers. Approach the cricket pavilion on the left and bear right to reach the bridge over the Goit. Dogs seem to know that this is the time to be released from the lead.

Pass **Black Coppice** and then a conifer plantation to the left to reach **Moor Road** and **Anglezarke reservoir**.

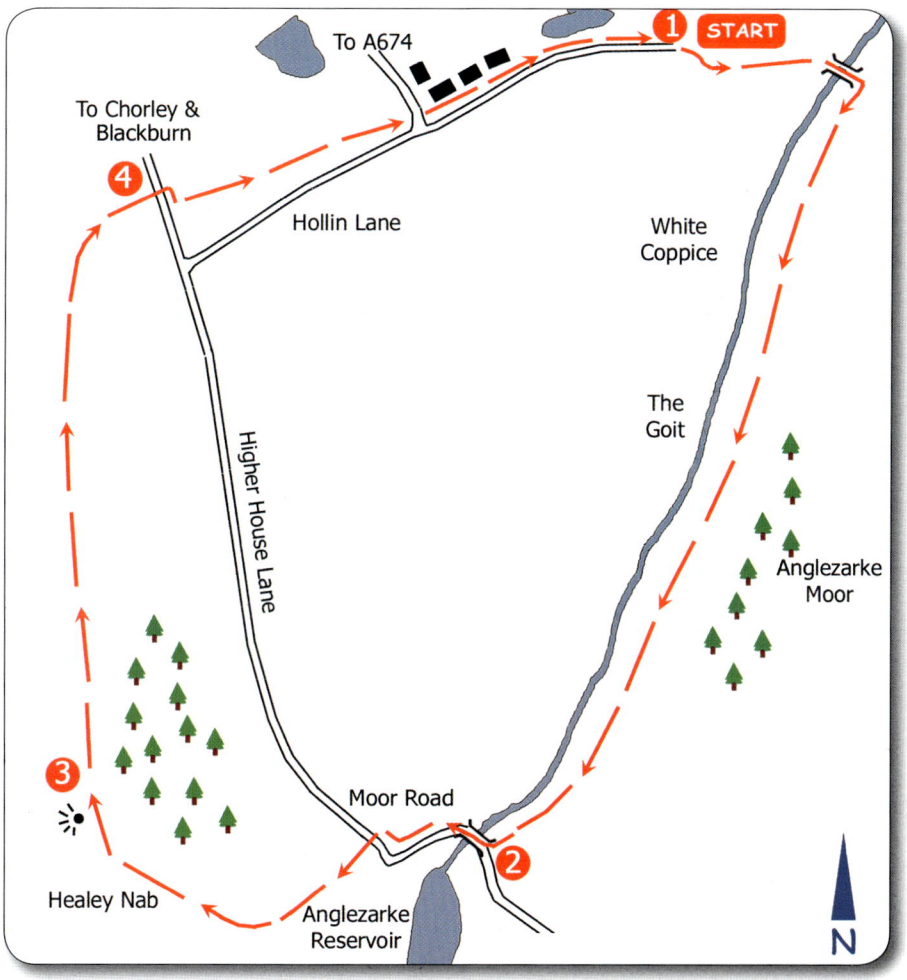

Lancashire – A Dog Walker's Guide

Black Coppice is mainly coniferous and is hence dark in contrast to White Coppice which has long been a place where silver birch trees dominate.

2 Turn right and walk for a short distance along Moor Road and then see a footpath and turn left. Look across the Anglezarke reservoir to see the old **Waterman's Cottage**. Here, especially in the cooler months, is the ideal time to look out for a variety of wildfowl. There is now a steep climb leading to a stile. Cross over this and follow an obvious track to reach a cairn which marks the summit of **Healey Nab**, at 682 ft (208m).

The area called Grey Heights is covered with gorse and heather and is the haunt of red grouse and short-eared owls. Here was once an area of quarries and the stone was of such a high quality that it was in demand all over the north-west of England during the time the cotton towns were evolving.

3 The path now sweeps to the right through an area of conifer-dominated woodland and here is a chance to catch your breath and enjoy a viewing point with panoramic and often spectacular scenery. This is excellent dog territory with lots of smells to slow them down and sticks to chase to speed them up! On good days there are views of Blackpool, Southport, Chorley and Parbold. Like any upland walk a time has to be chosen when visibility is good. Follow a wide and obvious track and then begin a steep descent through another area of woodland. Bear right to reach another easy to negotiate stile and pass through an area of lush meadowland to reach **Higher House Lane**. This is another excellent area to allow fit dogs to enjoy a good chase.

4 Turn right along Higher House Lane but only for about 200 yards. Look out for a footpath sign; turn left and cross a stile into a field. Bear right to another stile and continue straight ahead. At the road junction turn right and return to the starting point at **White Coppice**.

The cricket pavilion at White Coppice.

Around Healey Dell

The impressive viaduct.

Healey Dell, now the focus of a nature reserve and a pleasant visitor centre, is steeped in history so whilst your dog takes in the sounds and smells of the riverside, you can enjoy reflecting on the area's past. In Anglo-Saxon times this area was called Healey Thrutch – the word *thrutch* meaning a cutting through rocks eroded by a river, which in this case was the fast-flowing Spodden. The oak and birch woodland on the north bank of the river is thought to be a remnant of an ancient and once extensive forest. The Healey Hall estate has been a local landmark from at least medieval times when the De Heleya family were in residence. Along the way, you will also pass a massively impressive viaduct and aqueduct which is 200 ft long and supported on eight graceful brick-built arches.

Signs of the secret activities which took place in the dell during the Second World War are also on display. Here large concrete buildings were hurriedly constructed to store high explosives, guarded by members of the Home Guard. When the war ended, the lime-rich mortar left lying around proved ideal for plants such as orchids, rock rose and bird's foot trefoil to thrive.

In the centre of the dell, close to the Information Centre, is the Healey Dell Studios. This is open all year round and is a base for local artists, including a sculptor who specialises in portraits of dogs!

Where to park

At the Healey Dell Information Centre where there is free parking (GR SD882162). **OS map:** OL21 South Pennines.

How to get there

From Bacup follow the A671 towards Rochdale. Some 2 miles before reaching the town, look out for a sharp right-hand turn, signed to the nature reserve. Descend the very steep and winding road to reach the parking area and information centre.

Nearest refreshments

There is a variety of cafés and pubs in Bacup and Rochdale and plenty of quiet spots on the route to enjoy a picnic, so why not call in at Bacup and buy fresh bread and locally-sourced food from the market area. Don't forget to buy the dog biscuits!

The Walk

· ·

Before you set off from the Information Centre, take time to explore some of the buildings from the early years of the cotton industry, which date from around 1780. The mills were just that – old corn mills converted into textile factories. These mills were powered by the waters of the fast-moving River Spodden. Once towns such as Bacup and Rochdale developed steam-powered factories these old watermills proved to be uneconomic and one by one they closed.

Dog factors

· ·

Distance: 2 miles.
Road walking: Minimal.
Livestock: None.
Stiles: None.
Nearest vets: Valley Vetcare, Rochdale.

❶ Follow the wide track and pass an old mill pond on the right.

Look for the foundations of what were once the stores used in the Second World War. Away to the right and beyond the old railway line is Healey Hall.

❷ Cross the bridge over the **River Spodden** to reach the old railway line and follow the line along the obvious track, with the valley of the River Spodden and its wooded ravine below.

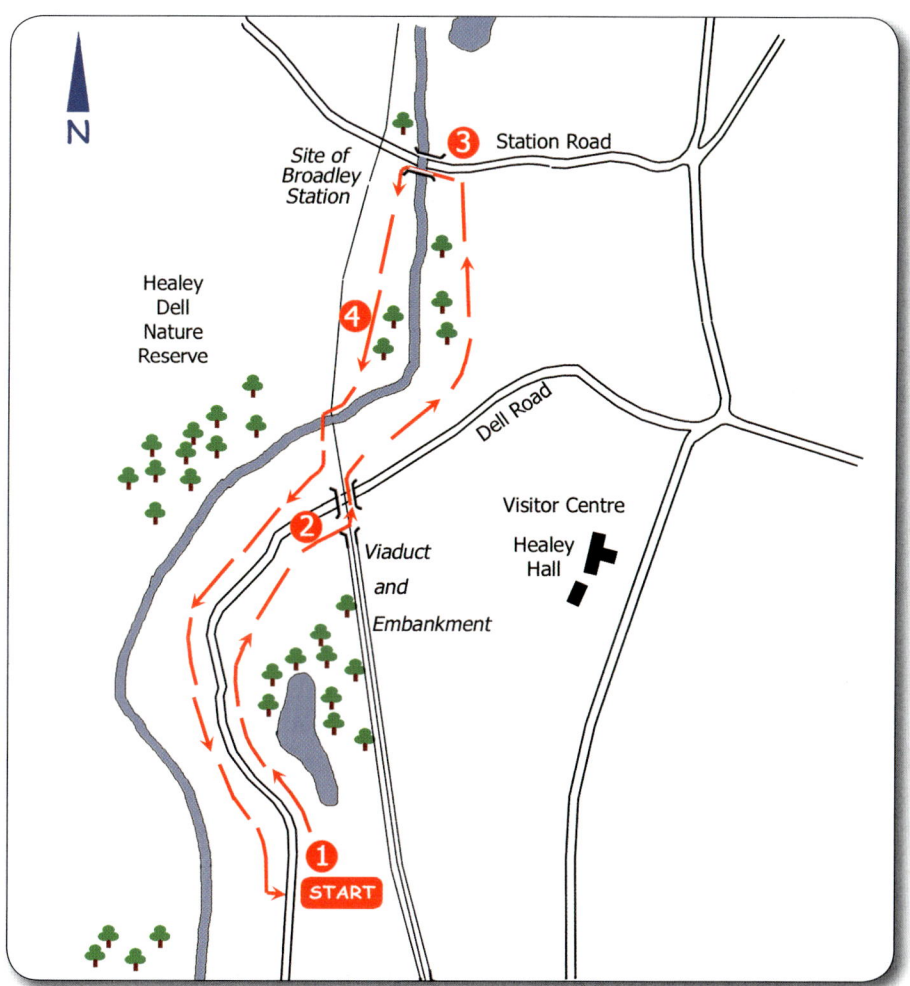

You are now in a dog's paradise. Here also is the Healey Dell Nature Reserve which was set up in 1976 and based around the steam-operated line which ran between Bacup and Rochdale. This was built around 1867 and closed 100 years later. The railway route was never very successful even in its prime and it was always a single-line track. There are records of the engine crews stopping on occasions to catch rabbits to supplement their wages. They set snares one day and collected the rabbits on the next.

A visit to the Healey Dell Studios is well worthwhile.

There is a great deal of folklore associated with the Spodden as it tumbles through narrow grottoes and over waterfalls. Legend has it that Robin of Locksley visited the dell to woo a young lady. Robin Hood's Well is still visited and it is said that our hero was almost, but not quite, lured to his death by a witch. Some of the rocks have been eroded by the water to produce human-like shapes and this no doubt helped to fuel the legend.

3 Approach and cross **Station Road** before turning left along a track between the railway and the river.

Here is the chance to explore what is left of the platform of Broadley station. Time should be taken here to let the dogs wander at will. They will not go very far away, especially if this area is chosen to enjoy your picnic!

4 Follow the old railway line to the viaduct, and return to the visitor centre and parking area.

There are several vantage points from where the river and the rocks which are found in its bed and waterfalls can be safely explored. Children can have lots of fun looking at the rocks to see how many human-like faces can be identified.

Holcombe Moor and Ramsbottom

A winter walk on Holcombe Moor.

The walk – and this is a walk rather than a stroll – begins at the Ramsbottom Steam Railway station. The East Lancashire Railway began operating in the 1840s but fell victim to stringent cuts in 1972. The line was rescued from the 1980s onwards and now runs from Rawtenstall via Ramsbottom, Bury and on to Heywood. Perhaps this is the perfect place for your dog to enjoy a trip on a steam train after the walk, and is a reminder of the good old days when most people took their pets with them and cars were very much a luxury form of transport. Dogs are welcome and can travel for free on the East Lancashire Railway. Check their website for timetables and fares: www.eastlancsrailway.org.uk

From the station we walk out onto the open moor and up to the Peel Monument, commemorating Sir Robert Peel, the man who founded the police force. This area is owned and as usual well-maintained by the National Trust. The monument stands on the moor at a height of 1,100 ft (335 m) above sea level. It is seen at its best from the steam railway line but there is a wonderful view from the monument down into the valley of the River Irwell. Passing an ancient Pilgrims' Cross, we return through woodland and alongside the river.

Lancashire – A Dog Walker's Guide

Those who enjoy the origin of the names of towns and villages will find lots of interest on this walk. Ramsbottom, for example, means *the valley where the wild garlic grows*. The Old English name for this plant was *Hramsa* so we originally had Hramsabottom.

Terrain

This is quite a strenuous walk with some steep ascents.

Where to park

The large car park close to the East Lancashire railway station from where the walk starts (GR SD792168). **OS map:** Explorer 287 West Pennine Moors.

How to get there

Turn off at junction 1 of the M66 and follow the A56 towards Ramsbottom. Follow the signs to Ramsbottom town centre along Bury New Road. Pass over the level crossing and then turn left to reach the car park.

Refreshments

There are plenty of pubs and restaurants in the area, including the Grant Arms Hotel in the centre of Ramsbottom (☎ 01706 823354).

The Walk

● ●

1 Turn left from the car park and follow **Railway Street**, ignoring a bend to the right. Look out on the left for a building used by a haulage company. This was once the Old Square Mill built by the Grant brothers in 1821. The road bends to the left but ignore this and follow a narrow path which twists first right and then left along a paved track leading to **St Andrew's church**.

The Grant brothers came from Scotland in the early 19th century and made their

> ## Dog factors
>
> ●
>
> **Distance:** 5½ miles.
> **Road walking:** About 1½ miles, not on main roads but mostly on tracks with some vehicle access.
> **Livestock:** Seldom if any.
> **Stiles:** 5, over one of which some dogs may need a little help.
> **Nearest vets:** Bonham Veterinary Centre, Ramsbottom.

fortunes from cotton. They were so well loved in Ramsbottom that they were visited by Charles Dickens, who was at that time working as a journalist. He featured them in his novel Nicholas Nickleby *in 1859, as the Cheeryble brothers. The church, dedicated to the Scottish patron saint, was built by the Grants in 1826. Hot air issuing from the Square Mill was piped to the church and kept it warm.*

Continue past the church to the main road and turn left. Look out for the **Old Dun Horse pub** and cross the road. Dogs need to be firmly under control at this point. Walk up **Dundee Lane** – yet another Grant association because the brothers originally hailed from this place.

Look out on the left for the old schoolhouse built in 1864. Incorporated into it are two fascinating features: the front porch came from the old courthouse at Helmshore and the date stone showing 1414 came from Manchester Cathedral, which was at that time a not very substantial parish church.

2 As **Dundee Lane** narrows look out for **Downfield Close** and then for a footpath, which leads to the **Shoulder of Mutton pub** in **Holcombe** village.

At a nearby old school look out for bullet holes in the wall which were the result of a German Zeppelin attack on the village in 1916.

Turn left along **Cross Lane** to find a footpath leading up to the Peel monument. This is the time to let dogs explore the open moorland and here it is possible to see the inquisitive pooch in action and call it back if necessary.

3 A very steep but obvious track leads to **Holcombe Moor** with the **Peel monument** close to the summit.

The Peel monument was erected in 1852 by public subscription to commemorate the life of Sir Robert Peel (1788–1850). He was killed by falling from his horse, but not before he had founded the police force: early constables were called 'Peelers' and then 'Bobbies'. He was also Prime Minister from 1834 to 1835 and then from 1841 to 1846.

From the Peel tower bear left across the moor and pass through a gate. After about a mile find the ancient **Pilgrims' Cross** on the right.

This was one of the many markers on the trail leading towards the Cistercian abbeys of Whalley and Sawley. Historians have shown that these crosses date from as early as 1166. All that remains of this cross now is a flat support stone and close by is a flagpole.

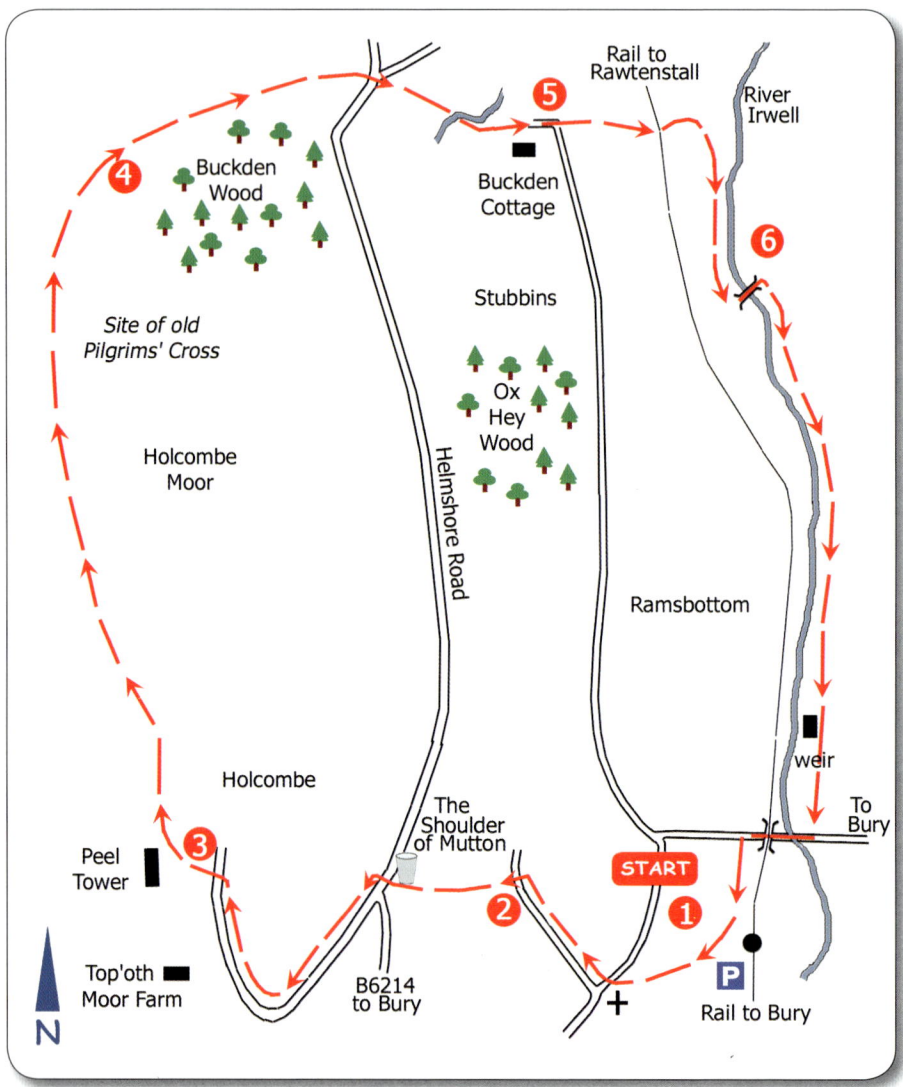

Continue and turn right and descend to reach a stile in a stone wall. Pass through this stile.

4 Enter **Buckden Wood**, a name implying that red and roe deer were once present in the area in some numbers.

Passing Ramsbottom station, with Peel Tower in the distance on the left.

The track widens to reach a substantial ladder stile, where some dogs may need a little help. The path then descends to **Helmshore Road**. Cross this to reach a substantial stile on the right. Pass through this and follow a fence down to the left. Cross two more stiles and a footbridge over a stream. Bear left and keep a stream on the left. Find **Buckden Cottage** to the right, having re-crossed the stream which is now to the right. This gives dogs the chance to have a splash. The obvious path now leads onto a narrow road.

5 Turn left and pass under two bridges, the second carrying the railway, and turn right along a narrow track. Look out for the old **Aitkens Mill** across the river.

6 Cross a bridge over the river and turn right. You are now in the old village of **Stubbins** which is divided into two by the railway and a road. The **River Irwell** is now on the right. Pass through a kissing gate and follow the path onto **Kenyon Street**. Turn right and cross the river, looking for the splendid old weir on the Irwell to the right. Go over the level crossing and turn left back to the starting point.

Smithills Country Park

The entrance to the Coaching House seen through the trees.

Here is a stroll to enjoy, packed with fascinating history, natural history and stunning scenery. For our canine companions there are smells and sounds guaranteed to provide both interest and exercise. Smithills Country Park, stretching over 2,000 acres, is a delight and the walk explores both woodland and riverside. On dull days with no wind the reflections in the water of the trees overlooking the half-timbered Coaching House are magnificent but this area is a scenic joy at all times. The original dwelling was built by the Knights Hospitallers in the 12th century and is set on a hill overlooking Ravenden Clough (a clough is a local name for a small river valley). This stroll winds its way around the clough and the brook which flows through it. As its name implies, ravens once nested on the slopes of the wooded ravine.

Dog factors
. . . .
Distance: 2 miles.
Road walking: None.
Livestock: None
Stiles: None.
Nearest vets: Pike Moor Vets, Horwich.

Parts of the present hall date from the 14th century but there have obviously been lots of alterations since that time. The medieval hall has some famous and magnificent quatrefoil decorations which have been dated to about 1350. Many of the rooms have well-preserved 16th-century carvings. The chapel attached to the house was burned down but rebuilt in 1856. In 1938 Smithills was bought by Bolton Corporation and has served as a museum ever since. For details of the opening times of Smithills Hall telephone 01204 332377.

Children may enjoy a visit to the open farm which is open daily (there is an entry fee) and offers close encounters with domestic animals and donkey and tractor rides; there are also deer kept in a large enclosure. Families could plan to walk the dog first, then visit the farm and perhaps walk the dog again because there is so much for them to enjoy.

Terrain
The terrain is easy and there are places for dogs to run free but they need to be on a lead when passing close to Smithills Hall and the Coaching House.

Where to park
There is free parking alongside Smithills Coaching House Café and parking for the disabled by the Hall (GR SD699119). **OS map:** Explorer 287 West Pennine Moors.

How to get there
From the A675 which links Blackburn with Bolton and close to Belmont turn off onto Scout Road, signposted Horwich, and then left onto Smithills Dean Road. Descend to reach a sign on the left indicating Smithills Hall and the parking area.

Refreshments
The Wilton Arms, Belmont Road, (☎ 01204 303307) serves delicious food and allows dogs at one end of the bar. It also has an outside seating area. There is a good café at the open farm and plenty of places to picnic.

Lancashire – A Dog Walker's Guide

The Walk

. . . .

1 Start at the **Coaching House** and pass through the impressive archway with its tower dominated by a clock.

In the cobbled yard look out for two restored coaches which once operated on the old turnpike road linking the expanding cotton towns of Blackburn and Bolton. Do not forget to look up to the upper area of the walls to see examples of the leather harnesses and all of the tack associated with the coaching era.

2 Patient hounds are now rewarded as a footpath sign indicates Smithills Hall and the Warden's Office. Descend to a substantial stone bridge. The bridge spans the stream, which then widens out to form a large pond. This is the place for dogs to explore the smells and for owners to enjoy a birdwatch and look out for treecreepers, jays and greater spotted woodpeckers.

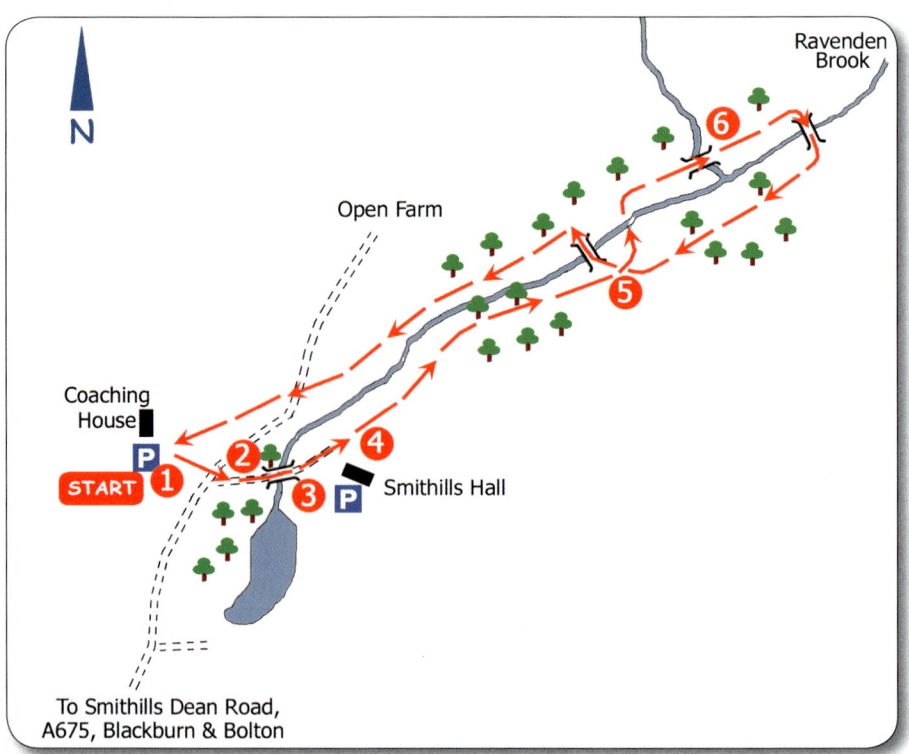

3 Ascend the gentle incline to **Smithills Hall** and the Ranger's Office. This is good easy walking and the track is neatly cobbled. This is the one place to put a dog on the lead.

4 Leaving the Hall behind, now is the area to 'let every dog have its day'. Follow the twists and turns of an obvious path which soon reaches an attractive little stone bridge.

In this area rare species of crane flies have been identified. Here too are some fine specimens of trees, especially beeches. When the Hall was self-sufficient the oil from the beech nuts was used as a furniture polish and the long sharp buds were used as toothpicks. Look out for stone walls which once marked the margins of the 19th-century gardens, including orchards and vegetable plots to supply the estate with home-grown food.

One of the restored coaches on display at Smithills.

5 Cross a tributary of **Ravenden Brook**.

This area is dominated in places by rhododendrons, which were planted to provide cover for the game birds such as pheasants which were another vital source of food. Another foreign import in this area is the Japanese knotweed which is an ever-present problem for those who have to manage the area. The cover of rhododendrons, however, is perfect habitat for inquisitive canines.

6 Cross another footbridge and turn sharp right through yet more woodland and along an obvious but continuously meandering track. Now cross another small footbridge over **Ravenden Brook** and then bear left. This is the place to look out for resident dippers and grey wagtails along the stream and for green woodpeckers which are found among the mature trees. Return to the **Coaching House** and the starting point.

APPENDIX

The following are all veterinary practices that are close to the walks described.

Abbeydale Veterinary Centre
91 Preston New Road, Blackburn BB2 6AY ☎ 01254 681811

Alison P. Lee Vets
2 Queen Street, Carnforth, LA5 9EB ☎ 01524 735249

Arcade Veterinary Centre
Windsor Park, Garstang PR3 1NS ☎ 01995 600606

Bay Veterinary Centre
194 Lancaster Road, Morecambe LA4 5TL ☎ 01524 410867

Bonham Veterinary Centre
Central Street, Ramsbottom, Bury BL0 9AF ☎ 01706 827787

Hillcrest Animal Hospital
Water Street, Chorley PR7 1EX ☎ 01257 262448

Mearley Veterinary Group
Holden Street, Clitheroe BB7 1LU ☎ 01200 423763

The Mount Veterinary Surgery
1 Harris Street, Fleetwood, FY7 6QX ☎ 01253 875547

'My Vet'
Myerscough House, Longsight Road, Clayton-le-Dale, Blackburn BB2 7JA
☎ 01254 814863

Oakmount Veterinary Centre
Oakmount House, Trafalgar Street, Burnley BB1 1TB ☎ 01282 423640

Pike Moor Vets
158–160 Chorley New Road, Horwich, Bolton BL6 5QW ☎ 01204 694004

Stanley House Veterinary Surgeons
14–18 Skipton Road, Barnoldswick BB18 5NB ☎ 01282 852390

Valley Vetcare
48 Whitworth Road, Rochdale, OL12 0EZ ☎ 01706 656559

Veterinary Health Centre
4 Greenways, Lytham St Annes FY8 3LY ☎ 01253 729309